First Prize

PIES

First Prize

PIES

SHOO-FLY,
CANDY APPLE &
OTHER DELICIOUSLY
INVENTIVE PIES FOR
EVERY WEEK OF THE YEAR
(AND MORE)

· ALLISON KAVE ·

PHOTOGRAPHS BY TINA RUPP

STEWART, TABORI & CHANG
NEW YORK

Published in 2014 by Stewart, Tabori & Chang

An imprint of ABRAMS

Text copyright © 2014 Allison Kave

Photographs copyright © 2014 Tina Rupp

Library of Congress Control Number: 2013945638

ISBN: 978-1-61769-102-7

Editor: Holly Dolce

Design and Illustration: Laura Palese

Production Manager: Tina Cameron

The text of this book was composed in Trixie, Calibre, and Icing.

Printed and bound in China

10 9 8 7 6 5 4 3 2 1

Stewart, Tabori & Chang books are available at special discounts when
purchased in quantity for premiums and promotions as well as fundraising
or educational use. Special editions can also be created to specification.
For details, contact specialsales@abramsbooks.com or the address below.

ABRAMS
THE ART OF BOOKS SINCE 1949

115 West 18th Street
New York, NY 10011
www.abramsbooks.com

FOR JAY

Table of Contents

INTRODUCTION

Thank you.

Before delving into the recipes, techniques, and personal stories of this pie-centric cookbook, I want to thank you, the reader, for giving me your time and attention. One thing I've learned in pursuing this dream is that pie is more than a dessert. It builds community, brings neighbors together, and sparks nostalgia and creativity. By reading and baking from this book, you continue that tradition, and I'm grateful to be part of it.

the kaves: food fanatics

I have an overwhelming passion for food. If I'm not cooking it, I'm talking about it, reading about it, writing about it, or just dreaming about it. This fixation didn't come out of nowhere—I give full credit to my culinary superstar of a mother, Rhonda Kave.

Decades before she founded her shop, Roni-Sue's Chocolates, in New York's Essex Street Market (which once served as the kitchen for First Prize Pies!), my mom was a homemaker looking to feed her kids nutritious meals while providing herself with a creative outlet. Her own mother's idea of cooking was to open a can of vegetables and boil them for an hour, so she had a lot of learning to do.

Her path to culinary knowledge was winding and global, and she took her family along for the ride. Some of my fondest childhood memories are of guacamole, Syrian flatbreads, hippie applesauce (unstrained and unsweetened, with the skins), and her sticky, delectable, blue-ribbon winning gingerbread. These are just a few of the healthy, from-scratch, delicious meals she prepared for us, and they opened my eyes to the different worlds we can access through food.

My brother, Corwin, was the first of us to dive into the professional culinary world. When he was in high school, my mom borrowed some Julia Child videos from the library, and he was soon re-creating her recipes at home. From there, it was a direct path to culinary school, and eventually he became executive chef of a number of restaurants in New York City (at an absurdly young age—the guy's a wunderkind). His incredibly refined palate and whimsical yet precise use of ingredients is hugely inspiring to me, and I'm happy to be learning from my little bro every day.

My mother's career progressed more circuitously. For over twenty years, she made truffles every winter for holiday gifts, with ever more elaborate flavors and an increasingly long list of recipients. When a spot became available in the Essex Street Market on New York's Lower East Side, she jumped at the chance. Now she's a full-time chocolatier and confectioner. Her fearlessness and courage in pursuing her dreams had an enormous impact on me.

A LIFETIME LOVE OF PIE

When my brother and I were little, our parents fell in love with flying. On the weekends we would find ourselves high above the clouds in their little Cessna, hopping between tiny regional airports. Despite the seeming glamour of such excursions, my brother and I quickly grew bored in the backseats of our plane, and would only be appeased with a stop at the Dutchess County Airport, whose little café had a chocolate cream pie that haunted our dreams. What on earth is better than cool, creamy chocolate pudding cradled by buttery pastry and topped with a mountain of vanilla whipped cream? For my brother and me, pretty much nothing.

Over time, it became clear that I would need to find my food niche in the family. Every Thanksgiving, we'd travel up to Vermont to ski (I mainly went for the clam chowder and hot cider). I soon started trying my hand at pie baking, for what is a Thanksgiving table without pie? Every year, I experimented, with varying success, but I always enjoyed myself. I discovered what makes pie so challenging, and ultimately so rewarding: You've gotta slow down. I think of pie making as a form of physical meditation; you're focused on just one thing, and it takes as long as it takes. You can't rush or cut corners, you can't

OPPOSITE (clockwise from top left): My mom, Rhonda, and me, age two (she still has that hat!). | My brother, Corwin, my mom, and me in Paris, 2013. | A very happy trip to Disney World! | Me and Mom, Christmas in Hong Kong.

be aggressive; you've got to relax, focus, and enjoy each step. For one who is not patient by nature (ahem, yours truly), it is a wonderful way to unplug.

Through all the crazy years of adolescence, college, and early adulthood, pie making was my weekly refuge. I'd spend a few hours each Sunday whipping up something new, letting the stresses of my life dissipate, and then I'd have a freshly baked pie to give. Do you know how popular you can become by giving away home-baked pies? Try it with a few of these, and you'll see.

FROM HOBBY TO CAREER

I wasn't always a baker. Just a few years ago, I wore heels and hose to work instead of clogs and an apron. I had a growing career in the art world, and lived in London for a while to get my master's degree. But no matter how well I did, or how successful I became, I always had a sense that it wasn't the right place for me. Every weekend, I'd escape to my kitchen and tune out all of the activity of the week and finally, there, I'd be happy.

My opportunity for change came in 2009, when an email popped up from my boyfriend, Jay, containing a link to the First Annual Brooklyn Pie Bake-Off, and a note of encouragement: "You should enter this. You will win." Now, let me say that I certainly didn't expect that to happen. I was confident in my pie abilities, to be sure, but there are *many* talented bakers in the borough of Brooklyn. I simply thought it would be a fun experience, and set about deciding which recipes to enter.

Jay caught the bug as well, and we wound up developing his recipe for Apple Cider Cream Pie (page 192) together. I entered with my signature recipe, Bourbon-Ginger-Pecan (page 170), and a very different version of my S'mores Pie (page 130). An incredibly enjoyable day was spent oohing and aahing over the more than forty pies that filled the table, and eating them, of course! At the end, Jay and I both walked out victorious: He took home Best Sweet Pie, and I left with the Best Overall Pie award for my beloved pecan.

It was such a crazy, fun experience, with all of my friends and family coming out to cheer me on, and it sparked an idea: Why not sell pie? I wasn't thinking large scale, and I certainly never thought it would be full time, but I talked to my mom about selling a few pies by the slice on the weekends at her shop and, as usual, she was behind me all the way. A couple of months later, I woke up to a write-up on the Web site Daily Candy, and my inbox was overflowing with orders. First Prize Pies was officially a *thing*. I was in the pie business.

After nearly three years of being the sole owner and operator of First Prize Pies, I teamed up with my partner, Keavy Blueher, owner of Kumquat Cupcakery here in New York. (See? Pie and cake *can* get along!) We had been friends for a while and participated in the same outdoor markets in Brooklyn (Smorgasburg and the Brooklyn Flea, which are *must-visit* places if you're traveling to New York!). We both were ready to end our nomadic ways and open a brick-and-mortar location. After much sangria and brainstorming, we came up with the concept for Butter & Scotch, our dessert and cocktail bar in Brooklyn, and the new home of First Prize Pies.

Pie is no longer just a hobby for me—it's my career, my craft, and I practice it pretty much every day. They say that you should never make a career of what you love, but I say they're crazy. I have never been more professionally or creatively fulfilled, and it thrills me to be able to share some of my recipes with my fellow bakers and food fanatics. I hope you enjoy baking them as much as I enjoyed creating them.

OPPOSITE (clockwise from top left): Slingin' pies for a good cause. | "P" is for Pie. | Me and Keavy (AKA Butter & Scotch). | A typical summer assortment at Smorgasburg.

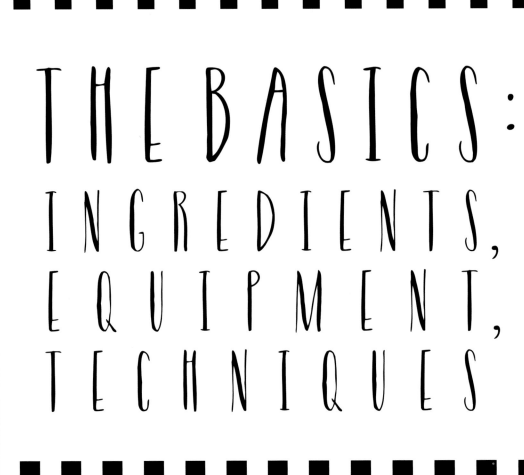

THE BASICS:
INGREDIENTS,
EQUIPMENT,
TECHNIQUES

Before diving into the pie recipes in this book, I encourage you to take some time to read through this introductory section, which will guide you through the most daunting part of pie making: the crust. It also contains lots of helpful tips regarding ingredients and equipment, including substitutions. This is the core foundation of pie baking, and knowing these techniques will make the whole process more fun and relaxing.

ingredients matter

For the most part, pies are made up of pretty simple ingredients. Flour, sugar, butter, salt, cream, and eggs form the backbone of most recipes. With such simple components, quality is of utmost importance. Here are a few of my key ingredients:

BUTTER

Without exception, I use high-quality, European-style butter in my pie crusts. Plugrá is a personal favorite, but anything with a high butterfat and low moisture content is what you're looking for. Your resulting crusts will be significantly more delicious, flaky, and tender. They will also be less likely to shrink, due to the butter's lower water content. Be sure to go for unsalted butter, which will allow you to precisely control the amount of salt in your recipes. Speaking of which . . .

SALT

Unless otherwise indicated, when I use the term "salt" in these recipes, I'm referring to fine, uniodized sea salt. I prefer its flavor, and it is easy to find at pretty much all grocery stores. If you don't have sea salt, you can substitute kosher salt, but will need to use about double the amount, as you get fewer grains of kosher salt per spoonful than sea salt. Avoid iodized table salt; it has a bitter aftertaste.

FLOUR

I always use unbleached, all-purpose flour for my pie crusts and fillings. It is less processed than bleached, enriched white flour, and yields consistent results. My two favorite brands are King Arthur and Hecker's.

SUGAR

When calling for sugar in this book, I am referring to white, granulated cane sugar. Recipes will otherwise specify a need for light brown or dark brown sugar, which are simply white sugar with different amounts of molasses incorporated. Recipes will also call for topping pie crusts with "raw sugar," by which I mean large-crystal turbinado or raw cane sugar.

EGGS

I use organically raised eggs in my pies, and find that it makes a big difference in both the flavor and texture of my custards. It's also the ethical option, both for the hens laying the eggs and for the ground they live on.

CREAM & MILK

I use organic milk and cream in my pies as well. At the very least, try to ensure that the dairy products you're using are free of the growth hormones that many industrial dairy farms are giving to their cows.

Spiced Fig Pie. For recipe, see page 150.

CHOCOLATE

I'm the daughter of a chocolatier—it stands to reason that I'll have some pretty strong opinions on the matter. The quality of your chocolate has a huge impact on the overall flavor of your finished recipe. Avoid the mass-produced, candy-bar style chocolates, which are full of oils, emulsifiers, and artificial flavor, and go for the best stuff you can get your hands on. My mom is a partner in Moho Chocolate, a direct-trade, bean-to-bar chocolate factory in Belize, so I'm lucky enough to use that for all my dark chocolate needs. I also love the flavor of Callebaut's milk chocolate.

MAPLE SYRUP

I use real maple syrup in most custards where corn syrup is traditionally called for. I love its flavor, and it's a healthier, less-processed ingredient. I always try to use Grade B, which is a richer, darker, more strongly flavored grade of syrup.

THICKENERS

There is much debate about the best way to absorb the juices in fresh fruit pies, which can become runny messes if not properly handled. Some like flour, others tapioca, while I'm a cornstarch girl myself. I find it thickens reliably, stays clear (unlike flour, which clouds the juices), and doesn't become over-gelled the way tapioca sometimes can.

BOOZE

I've been tending bar on and off over the past decade, and have a real appreciation for quality spirits. I've long been a proponent of incorporating liquor into desserts, as even a small amount can greatly elevate a recipe and give it a more nuanced, sophisticated flavor. Be sure to use the good stuff!

HERBS

I like to approach pastry recipes the way I approach savory ones: Widen the field of potential ingredients and flavors, and fantastic results will follow. For example, I like to use fresh herbs in some of my pie recipes to give them another layer of flavor. Feel free to experiment with different herbs that appeal to you; just be aware of their potency and don't overdo it.

NUTS

A number of recipes in this book call for toasted nuts. I generally toast nuts on the stovetop: In a clean, dry, heavy skillet, heat an even layer of nuts over medium-low heat, shaking the pan every once in a while, until they are fragrant but not burnt. Keep a close eye on them, as it's easy to go too far.

MERINGUE

Meringue is an essential component of chiffon pies, and is also used as a topping, as in my Cranberry Dream Pie (page 176). They can be finicky to make, but a few tips will ensure good results. Cold eggs separate more easily and cleanly, but room-temperature whites make the most voluminous meringues, so separate eggs while they're cold (make sure not to let any yolk get in the whites!), then let the whites come fully to room temperature. Use only spotlessly clean bowls, ideally metal (copper is the best) or glass, never plastic. Wipe the inside of the bowl with a little lemon juice or vinegar to remove any trace of oil. Adding a bit of cream of tartar will help to stabilize the foam, and using superfine sugar will help it to more fully dissolve into the meringue. Beat the whites until they're glossy and form stiff peaks, then stop—they can become grainy if overbeaten. Be sure to spread the meringue all the way to the edges of the pie crust to prevent it from shrinking. Finally, adding meringue to hot, freshly baked pie fillings helps to prevent "weeping," the watery layer between the filling and the meringue.

tools of the trade

I am hardly a snob when it comes to gadgets. In a pinch, I've rolled out pie dough with wine bottles.
Pie is a rustic dessert that can be made from very humble ingredients, in very humble settings.
Take these as guidelines, for when you're ready to trick out your arsenal of baking tools.

SCALE

If you get nothing else on this list, get a scale. Pastry differs from savory cooking in that precision really matters, especially with an ingredient like flour, whose weight can vary drastically depending on how you put it in your measuring cup. I find that using a simple kitchen scale (it doesn't have to be digital, though those have their benefits) leads to reliable results, time and time again. Plus, there are some really cool-looking ones out there!

TORCH

I'm putting this second on my list because I'm obsessed. I think I might have a touch of the pyro in me, because I will never get tired of using my blowtorch. If you plan on baking meringue pies, or that s'mores pie, or crème brûlée, or you want to add a little color to a pan of glazed veggies, you can justify owning a torch—mostly because they're just so fun. Mine is from a company called Iwatani, which uses replaceable butane canisters. Unlike propane, the butane doesn't impart any flavor to the surface of your food. If you do decide to buy one, avoid the tiny models you see at specialty food stores. These are very weak and tend to die out pretty quickly. They're also overpriced.

BENCH SCRAPERS

You may not have these lying around the house, but bench scrapers are among the most versatile, useful kitchen tools you can own. I use mine to gently pry dough off of countertops, to clean off my work surfaces, to cut butter, and to make pie dough. I always have two on hand. I prefer the ones pictured, which have sturdy metal panels and easy-to-grip plastic handles. My preferred runner-up to these when making pie dough is a . . .

PASTRY BLENDERS

There are two types of pastry blenders out there: those with thin, round strands of metal, and those with thick, blade-like pieces of metal. You want the latter. These will more quickly and easily cut through the fats you're blending into your flour.

ROLLING PINS

There are two main types of rolling pins. The traditional American-style pins are usually made of wood or marble, and have a round cylinder that spins, with one handle on each end. French-style pins are long dowels that are thicker in the middle and taper at the ends. I greatly prefer the French pin, which I feel gives more control and rolls more evenly. Try them both, and see what's more comfortable for you.

PIE PLATES

Which to use? Glass, ceramic, aluminum—they all have their place. I use the light, disposable aluminum tins every day when baking whole pies for customers. Pies tend to bake more quickly in these inexpensive tins, and you don't have to worry as much about the bottom crust being underbaked.

Glass pie plates are prettier to look at, and the transparent sides and bottom allow you to clearly see when your crust has turned golden. They are thicker than the aluminum tins, and therefore generally need a bit more baking time.

Ceramic plates are beautiful, but I'd argue that they're best for experienced pie bakers, who can gauge when the pie is ready without needing to see the bottom crust. The thicker walls of these plates mean that even for fresh fruit pies, you might need to blind-bake the bottom crust first so it finishes at the same time as your filling. You can also help ensure a well-baked bottom crust by putting this dish on the floor of your oven in the last fifteen minutes of baking.

BAKING SHEETS

Baking sheets prevent a lot of disasters on the way from the counter to the oven. If you've got a jiggly custard crust, those spills are going to wind up on the baking sheet instead of all over your floor. If you've got a fruit pie that just can't help but bubble over, those juices will wind up on a much easier-to-clean surface than the bottom of your oven! Most of all, baking sheets help your pies to bake evenly and make them easier to move around, rotate, and safely handle. I recommend getting sturdy, heavy-duty half sheet pans, which fit most home ovens.

PAN LINERS

I always line my baking sheets, as I'm a klutz and invariably wind up spilling or dripping something as I fill my pie shells. I also find that fresh fruit pies often bubble over (which is beautiful, but messy), and their sticky juices can be a real pain to clean off of baking sheets. I like to line my pans with nonstick silicone or Teflon sheets; Silpats are wonderful and last forever. You can also use parchment.

BLIND-BAKING

We'll cover the technique of blind-baking in the next chapter, but there are a few tools that make the process much easier. After much trial and error, I've found that aluminum foil is the best material for lining your pie crust when blind-baking. It is easier to shape to the contours of your crust, and it helps to hold up the sides of the dough while they bake.

When it comes to pie weights, you can spring for the ceramic beads that you find at cooking supply stores, but they're expensive, and you really need three or four packages of them for a single pie. It's important to fill the cavity of the pie shell all the way up when blind-baking, and they never give you enough. Instead, I use dried beans or chickpeas, which you can use over and over again, storing them in a sealed jar. Just keep in mind that these get a bit stinky after a few uses, but they won't affect the flavor of your pie.

PIE SHIELDS

Pie shields are designed to cover the outer edge of your pie crust, to prevent it from getting too dark while the filling sets. You don't generally need them too often, but they can come in handy. This is another case in which I feel the manufactured product just doesn't do the job. I have yet to find a designated pie shield that securely hugs and covers the rim of the crust. Instead, I cut a large piece of aluminum foil, place the whole pie directly in the center, and roll the edges of the foil up to hug and cover the crust, while keeping the middle exposed. This method is sturdier and more adaptable, and the shield holds its place even in convection ovens.

CUTTERS

These are a few fun items you can invest in to achieve decorative top crusts. Something as simple as a fork can give you beautiful pie crusts, so don't think of these as necessities, but they can yield some very pretty results. Cookie cutters, which are inexpensive and easy to find (I especially love to dig up cool vintage ones), can be used to give a festive or seasonal accent to pie crusts. I also love my wheel cutter, which has a crimped edge that gives lattice crusts a quaint, rickrack-like appearance.

CANDY THERMOMETERS

My candy thermometer of choice is a digital model by Polder that has a built-in alarm to let you know when your caramel or syrup has reached the desired temperature. After many burnt pots of caramel, my boyfriend gifted me with one of these, and I'm now their biggest fan. You can also use them to test the temperature of roasting meats, and they have a built-in timer as well.

OVEN THERMOMETER

You set your oven to 350 degrees, so it's at 350 degrees, right? Probably not. Ovens tend to vary wildly in temperature, and heat is usually distributed unevenly. An oven thermometer will ensure that you're baking at the right temperature.

FREEZER

Marlene, my boyfriend's mom, has a secret for making Thanksgiving a bit less stressful: She bakes her pies in September, and half her work is done when it's time for the big dinner. The freezer can be a good pie baking ally. Certain pies can be baked ahead and frozen (generally, double-crust pies—such as apple and summer fruit—as well as pumpkin and pecan pies), and you can keep big batches of dough on hand for when the mood strikes. Be warned that custard pies should not be frozen—the filling will break and you'll be left with a sad puddle where your delicious custard should be.

the almighty crust

Crust is a pie baker's point of pride. It's the standard by which we're judged, and a good baker is always experimenting with new proportions, techniques, and dough recipes.

It's good to start with a basic crust recipe. This is the one that you'll turn to, time and again, for berry pies in the summer and apple pies in the fall. Once you've got this crust under your belt, there's not much you can't do, pie-wise.

Regardless of which recipe you choose, there are a few cardinal rules you'll need to follow to achieve that perfectly flaky, tender, gorgeous crust:

Rule 1: Keep it cold.

I'm not going to get too scientific on you, but the main goal with pie dough is to avoid developing too much gluten. You need gluten for the dough to hold together, but too much and you wind up with tough, brittle crust. One way to inhibit gluten development is to keep your ingredients as cold as possible. I make a habit of keeping my flour and butter in the freezer, so they're ready whenever I need to whip up a ball of dough.

Rule 2: Don't overwork it.

Pie is not pasta. Again, it all comes down to gluten. The more you handle and work the dough—the more you roll it around, knead it, and put your hands on it—the tougher your crust will be. Treat your dough gently, touch it as little as possible, and please don't knead it.

Rule 3: Keep it chunky.

I use the term *chunky* both literally and figuratively. You want to have actual chunks of butter in there: tiny little nuggets of goodness that will melt and puff up as the crust bakes. When you roll out your dough, it should be speckled with little dots of butter, like a beautiful piece of marble. You also want your dough to have a good amount of fat. Fat equals flavor, as we've all been told, but fat is also one of the keys to flaky, tender crust.

|||||||||||||||||||||||||||||||||||||||

EGG WASH

1 egg

1/4 cup water

Stir together to combine, then lightly brush over the exposed surface and edges of your pie crust. (I prefer silicone brushes, which won't shed bristles onto your lovely pie!) You can see my Sugar Plum Pie on page 140 for an example.

|||||||||||||||||||||||||||||||||||||||

Rule 4: Don't beat yourself up.

I intend for the recipes in this book to be as fail-proof as possible. That said, the more you practice the craft of baking, the better you'll become, and your first efforts may not be as flawless as you'd hope. I am my own harshest critic, and I know what it's like to want to toss your less-than-perfect pie in the trash. Hold back, take a breath, and give someone a slice. They're sure to sing your praises, and you can use this setback as a learning experience for the next pie.

Now that you've got the ground rules, let's bake!

DOUGH-BASED CRUSTS ELEMENTS

••

I'm going to break down the different components of my crust recipes here, so you can see the logic behind why I've chosen these particular ingredients, and how I use them.

FLOUR

You'll notice that most of the measurements listed are by weight. When it comes to butter, it is less crucial to use a scale, though I prefer it. When it comes to flour, weighted measurements are more important, as using measuring cups is very unreliable. However, if you're without a scale, there's one method that is best for measuring flour by volume:

Using a fork or spoon, fluff the flour in your bag or jar so it aerates and is not densely packed. Then, spoon the flour into your measuring cup until it's overflowing, and use a knife or other straight edge to level the surface. This will yield a cupful of flour weighing approximately 4 ounces (115 g).

BUTTER

As I mentioned at the beginning of the chapter, I use high-butterfat, European-style unsalted butter in my pie crusts. Try it up against your regular American table butter and you'll see a huge difference. When preparing the butter, I like to cut it into ½-in/12-mm cubes with a bench scraper or sharp knife. Then I cover the cubes in some plastic wrap and keep them in the freezer until I'm ready to make my crust.

CORNSTARCH

After a lot of testing, I discovered that adding just a bit of cornstarch to my pie dough yields a more tender crust. It's not crucial; you can leave it out if you don't have it (or if you have a corn allergy), but it helps to guarantee good results.

WHOLE MILK AND VINEGAR

You may have noticed by now that I like to keep the fat content of my pie dough rather high. Again, this is all in the interest of achieving the flakiest, most tender crust possible. To that end, instead of just using water, I find that using whole milk, soured with a bit of apple cider vinegar, makes an astonishing difference in your end result.

MAKING DOUGH BY HAND VS. USING A FOOD PROCESSOR

••

I love to make pie dough with my hands. It's relaxing, and you are physically connected to the process of creating your pie. That said, sometimes we're in a hurry. Sometimes we have to make a ton of dough. Sometimes we're just not in the mood. And I'm here to tell you, that's OK. You can get wonderful results by making dough in a food processor. In fact, it's harder to overwork the dough this way because the process is so speedy. For each crust recipe, I will include instructions for both methods, so you'll have your choice of slow and soothing, or quick and efficient.

ROLLING, CRIMPING, LATTICES & BLIND-BAKING

ROLLING

It's important to let your dough rest on the counter for about five minutes before you start to roll it. This will allow it to warm up just a bit, so it's easier to handle and less likely to crack.

Use lightly floured hands to gently shape the dough into a round disk. Lightly flour your clean work surface, lay down your dough, and then lightly flour the top of the dough as well as your rolling pin.

Starting from the middle of the disk, and using the weight of your body to press down on the dough, roll upwards, then downwards, rotating the dough a bit between every pass of the rolling pin. By moving the dough around as you roll, you'll maintain a round shape and uniform thickness, and you'll prevent the dough from sticking to your work surface. If you feel the dough start to stick, gently pry it off using a bench scraper or butter knife, then dust a bit more flour on your work surface.

Every once in a while, your dough will crack or split while you're rolling it. Don't freak out! Pie crust is more forgiving than you might think. Just tear a smidge of dough from the outer edge of your circle, and gently press it into the crack. Then sprinkle a tiny bit of flour over the patch, and roll it in. It will bake up just fine.

When the dough is about 10 inches (25 cm) in diameter and ⅛ to ¼ inches (3 to 6 mm) thick, you're ready to transfer it to your pie plate. You can help prevent the crust from sticking by lightly buttering your pie dish, especially on the bottom.

1. Lay rolling pin horizontally across the top of your dough.

4. Roll the pin backwards so your dough loops loosely around the rolling pin.

2. Roll upwards, then downwards, rotating the dough a bit during every pass.

3. To transfer your dough to a pie plate, lift the top edge of the dough up over the pin.

5. Bring the dough over to your pie plate and roll it off into place.

6. For double-crust pies, press the dough down into the dish, pushing it firmly into the bottom corners. Trim overhang with kitchen shears to 1 inch. For single-crust pies, fold overhang underneath itself and press firmly to seal it. Fill the pie, brush the edges with egg wash, and top it with a second crust.

LATTICE CRUSTS

Nothing looks better on a cherry pie than a beautiful lattice. Personally, I'm partial to thick-cut lattice strips, about 2 inches/ 5 cm, but you can weave a lattice with whatever size strips you like. People are often intimidated by this process, but with a bit of patience it's quite simple.

To begin, roll out a disk of pie dough into an 11-inch (28-cm) circle, about ¼ inch (6 mm) thick. Using a wheel cutter or paring knife, cut an even number of vertical strips out of the dough, at least six. You can use a ruler or measuring tape to make perfectly even strips, eyeball it, or make a bunch of different-size strips; it's totally up to you.

Fill the pie dough in your pie plate with whatever filling you're using, and then lay one strip across the center of your filling. Lay another strip across the middle, perpendicular to the first strip. Then lay two strips perpendicular to that strip, on either side. Peel back one side of the bottommost strip, lay a strip down perpendicular to that one, and cover it. Repeat on the other side. Continue this weaving process until you've used all your strips of dough, and the surface of your pie is covered.

For an alternative look, layer the lattice strips on a diagonal, still following the steps above.

Trim the edges to line up with the overhang of your bottom crust. Brush the rim with egg wash or milk, then you can either roll the dough under against the edge of your pie plate, or roll the overhang up over the edge of the lattice. The former technique gives a more rustic look, while the latter is a bit more polished. Crimp the edges using one of the techniques outlined below, and brush the lattice strips with egg wash or milk. Sprinkle with raw sugar.

1. Using a wheel cutter or knife, cut (relatively!) even strips of dough (at least 6).

4. Then, lay another strip perpendicularly on top, down the center.

2. Keep the lattice strips handy, and put your fruit filling in the bottom crust. Brush the exposed edges with egg wash or milk.

3. Start by laying one lattice strip down the center of your pie filling.

5. Lay two more strips parallel to, and on either side of, the bottom-most strip.

6. Gently peel back the bottom-most strip...

7. And add a perpendicular strip underneath.

8. Replace the folded-back strip.

9. Repeat the process on the other side.

10. Trim the excess lattice dough.

Fluted edge: a classic.

CRIMPING

I generally opt for a rustic, hand-crimped edge for my pies. I like people to see that my pies were made by hand. You can also use a fork or cookie cutters to create decorative edges. Be sure to keep your hands or tools floured as you proceed. Here are a few different techniques:

Fluted edge This is the most classic of crimping techniques, and easy to achieve. Place the index finger of your writing hand on the inner edge of your pie dough. Using the thumb and index finger of your other hand, gently squeeze the dough around that finger. Continue in a circle all the way around.

Rope edge This yields a beautiful rustic edge reminiscent of twisted rope. Using your writing hand, press down diagonally on the edge of the dough with your bent index finger, and use your thumb to gently pinch the dough up against the side of your finger. Repeat this in a circle all the way around.

Fork-crimped edge This is an easy way to get a pretty crust. Using a floured fork, gently press its tines down into the edge of the dough all the way around the pie. You can alternate the directions of the tines to get a pretty herringbone pattern. You can also flute the edge as above, and press your fork down into the center of each flute.

Cutout edge This is a bit fancier than the crimped edges above, and really gives pies an elegant, professional look. Roll out the scraps of dough that you trimmed off of your overhang until they're fairly thin. Cut shapes out of the scraps using a knife or crimped roller, or use a circular, square, or heart-shaped cutter (or any small cutter that strikes your fancy). Brush the edge of the pie dough with egg wash or milk, and arrange the cutouts along the rim, pressing them down lightly to adhere.

Crimp decoratively and brush with egg wash or milk.

A simple table fork is a great tool for a rustic-looking crust.

BLIND-BAKING

Blind-baking refers to the practice of baking a pie crust without its filling, and is an important technique in pie making. I recommend blind-baking whenever you have a filling that bakes more quickly than your crust (custards, for example), and also to prevent soggy bottom crusts. If you're baking in a thick-walled ceramic pie plate, even if the recipe doesn't call for it, you might want to blind-bake the bottom crust so it's nice and golden when you slice it. The method for blind-baking crumb crusts is different, and will be covered in the next chapter.

Preparing your dough for blind-baking Pie dough will not adhere to the walls of your pie plate without something to hold it up while baking. To blind-bake, roll the dough out into a circle, about 11 inches (28 cm) in diameter, and ⅛ to ¼ inch (3 to 6 mm) thick. Trim the overhang to 1 inch (2.5 cm), roll the overhang under and press it against the inner wall of the pie pan. Crimp decoratively (see page 34 for techniques). Make sure your crust is nice and cold (after rolling, return it to the fridge for at least 15 minutes, or better yet, the freezer). Prick the bottom of your unbaked crust all over with a fork (this helps to prevent it from shrinking). Line the dough with foil, making sure it is pressed down tightly into the bottom corners and against the sides, and roll the extra foil over the crimped edge of your crust to shield it. Fill the cavity with weights that will not burn in the heat of the oven. You can use the ceramic weights sold at most cooking stores, or simply buy some dried beans or peas, which are much more economical and can be reused. Be sure to use enough weights to fill the pie cavity up to the top.

Par-baking vs. fully blind-baking You'll see that some of the recipes in this book call for par-baking, and others for fully blind-baking. Par-baked crusts are not totally baked, as they will be returned to the oven with their filling. Fully blind-baked crusts are called for when the filling does not need to be baked, such as in pudding pies or caramel pies.

Line the dough with foil, and fill the cavity with dried peas or beans.

To par-bake, preheat the oven to 425°F (220°C). Prepare your chilled crust for blind-baking as described above. Bake for 20 minutes, rotating the pan once halfway through. Remove it from the oven, let it sit for a minute, and then carefully lift the weight-filled foil out of the crust, setting it aside to cool. If the bottom of your crust still appears buttery or wet, lower the temperature to 350°F (175°C) and return it to the oven for about 5 minutes, or until the bottom of your crust is dry but not golden. If the bottom of your crust puffs up in the oven, gently pat it down while it's still hot to release the trapped steam. Brush the edge of your crust with egg wash or milk, and follow the recipe instructions for filling and baking.

To fully blind-bake, follow the instructions for par-baking, remove the pie weights and foil, brush the edge of your pie crust with egg wash or milk, then return the unfilled pie to a 350°F (175°C) oven for 10 to 20 minutes, until the crust is fully baked and golden.

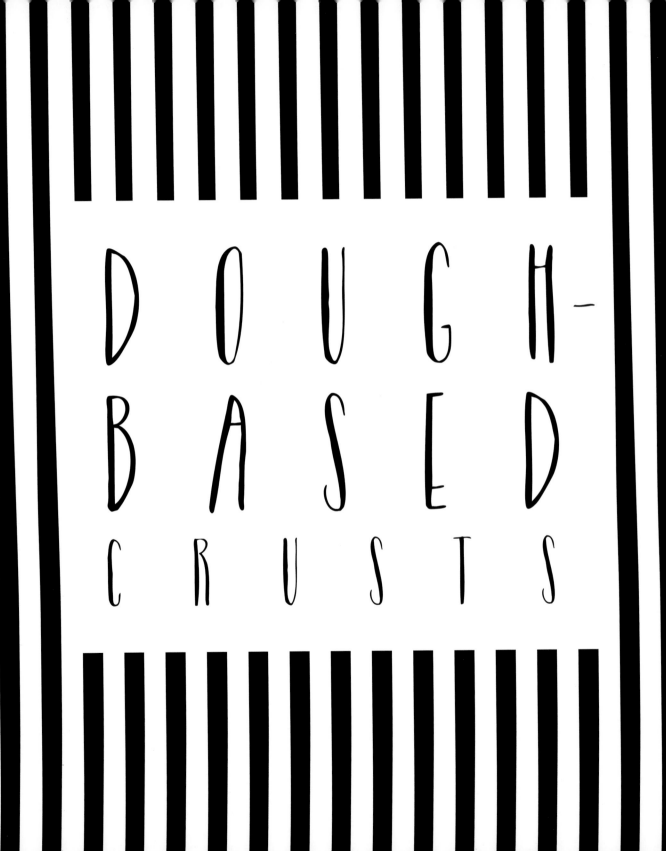

DOUGH-
BASED
CRUSTS

In this section, I'll provide recipes for dough-based pie crusts such as the classic pâte brisée (pie dough), cornmeal crust, chocolate crust, and even a vegan version. These are the fundamental crusts that you'll wind up using for most fruit, nut, and chocolate pies, as well as some custard pies.

I like my crusts to be well seasoned. Pie is unique in the dessert world as it's inherently savory and sweet. There's nothing like a forkful of salty, buttery, flaky crust with sweet, gooey filling. That contrast is what makes pie delicious.

CLASSIC PIE CRUST

My go-to pie crust has undergone a lot of changes over the years. This recipe is as close to perfect as I've been able to find. You can use all butter, or you can replace some of the butter with leaf lard or trans fat—free shortening, which will give you a surefire flaky crust without sacrificing buttery goodness.

As with all simple recipes, both the quality and treatment of your ingredients are paramount. I use unbleached all-purpose flour and add a little cornstarch, which helps to ensure a tender, flaky crust. I use a European-style cultured butter, which is higher in butterfat than most American butters, and its lower water content and rich buttery flavor result in a more reliable and more delicious crust. If you're using lard to replace some of the butter, try to get your hands on some leaf lard. It's the superfine lard from around the pig's kidneys. It has the lightest, least-porky flavor, and will guarantee you an incredibly flaky, tender pie crust. I avoid shortening; I'm just not a fan of putting such highly processed ingredients in my pie dough. However, if you want to use shortening, be sure to get one with no trans fats.

To bind the dough together, instead of water I use organic whole milk, which I sour with a little apple cider vinegar. Again, this is all about adding fat (which is synonymous with flavor!) and keeping the water content down, which helps prevent your crust from shrinking and helps it stay nice and flaky.

Lastly, the most important thing to remember is to keep your ingredients COLD, and to avoid overworking the dough while you're making it. I keep my flour in the freezer so it's ready at all times, and after cutting my butter into cubes, I put it back in the fridge to cool down for a few minutes before using.

In the Tools of the Trade section (see page 20), you'll see reference to some of the tools and techniques I use to make my dough. These are the tools that work best for me, but if your grandma taught you to make your dough using a fork, and that's how you like to do it, go for it. You can also use a food processor, which works beautifully. Those instructions are below this recipe.

This should be a fun, soothing, and meditative process that is full of enjoyment, so do what feels right!

MAKES enough for one double-crust 9-inch (23-cm) pie

³/₄ cup (1¹/₂ sticks/170 g) unsalted European-style cultured butter

¹/₄ cup (55 g) rendered leaf lard OR additional butter

¹/₂ cup (120 ml) whole milk

1 tablespoon apple cider vinegar (or any light-colored, mild vinegar)

12 ounces (340 g/ approximately 3 cups; see Note) unbleached all-purpose flour (chilled)

1 tablespoon cornstarch

2 tablespoons sugar

1¹/₂ teaspoons salt

Prepare the butter and lard, if using. Cut the butter into ½-inch (12-mm) cubes (a bench scraper is perfect for this, but a sharp knife works well too), and cut the lard into small pieces. Return them to the fridge or freezer to cool.

In a liquid measuring cup, stir together the milk and vinegar. Refrigerate the mixture until ready to use.

On a clean flat surface or in a large shallow bowl, toss the flour, cornstarch, sugar, and salt together lightly to blend. Add the butter and lard (if using) to the dry ingredients and, using the tool of your choice (see Tools of the Trade, page 20), cut the fat into the flour with speed and patience, until the fat has been reduced to small pea-sized chunks. Try to use a straight up-and-down motion, avoiding twisting your wrists, as the more you press on the flour the more tough gluten will develop in the dough. Avoid using your fingers, as the heat from your hands will melt the fat and further encourage gluten development. Unlike with pasta or bread, gluten is the enemy of pie dough, so be gentle, and be quick!

Once your fat has been cut down to size, spread your mixture out gently to expose as much surface area as possible. Gently drizzle about half of your milk mixture over the flour, trying to cover as wide an area as you can. Using bench scrapers or a large spoon, toss the flour over the liquid (don't stir; just lightly toss), spread everything out again, and repeat the process with the second half of the liquid.

You should now have a dough that will just hold together when pressed against the bowl, with visible little chunks of butter. If you need to add more liquid to bind it, do so with more cold milk, adding a tablespoon at a time until you reach the right texture. It's not an exact science, as everything from the humidity in the air to the dryness of your flour will affect the consistency of your dough.

Once you've reached your goal, cover the dough tightly in plastic wrap and refrigerate it for at least 1 hour. The dough can be kept in the fridge for up to 1 week, well wrapped, or in the freezer for up to 2 months.

NOTE See page 26 for flour-measuring instructions.

Food Processor Instructions

Prepare the butter, lard, and milk mixture as instructed above.

In the work bowl of a food processor fitted with a metal blade, add the dry ingredients and pulse once to blend. Remove the lid and add the fat. Replace the lid, have your milk mixture ready, and turn on the processor. After a couple of seconds, start to slowly pour the milk down the feed tube of the processor. As soon as all the milk has been added, turn off the machine. Pour the dough onto plastic wrap, bind it tightly, and refrigerate it for at least 1 hour.

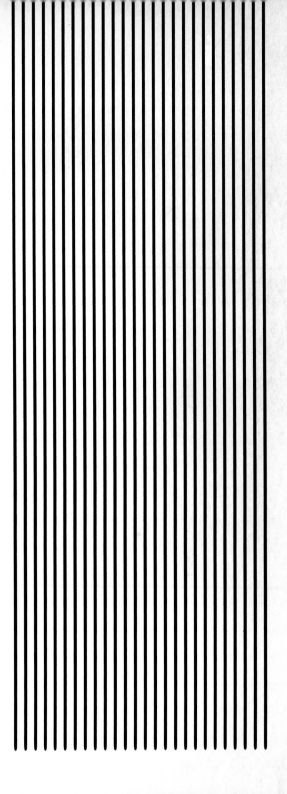

1. Cut cold butter into ½-inch cubes.

2. Add vinegar to cold milk.

5. Slowly drizzle in the milk mixture.

6. Toss the ingredients gently to combine.

3. Add butter to dry ingredients.

4. Chop the butter into pea-sized chunks.

7. Form a loose disk with your hands.

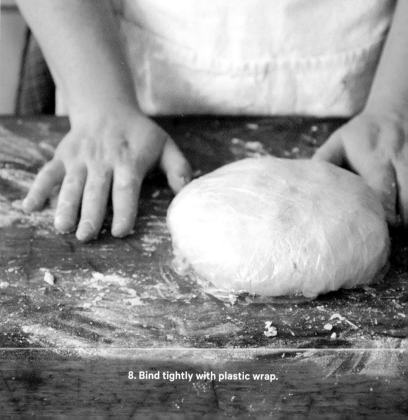

8. Bind tightly with plastic wrap.

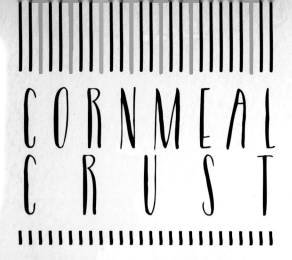

CORNMEAL CRUST

This crust has a more grainy, toothsome texture than a classic crust, and the natural sweetness of cornmeal makes a great accompaniment to summer pies such as blueberry or cherry. Use this when you want a truly rustic pie.

MAKES enough for one double-crust 9-inch (23-cm) pie

$^3/_4$ cup (1$^1/_2$ sticks/170 g) unsalted European-style cultured butter

$^1/_4$ cup (55 g) rendered leaf lard OR additional butter

$^1/_2$ cup (120 ml) whole milk

1 tablespoon apple cider vinegar (or any light-colored, mild vinegar)

9 ounces (255 g/ approximately 2$^1/_4$ cups) unbleached all-purpose flour (chilled)

3 ounces (85 g/approximately $^3/_4$ cup) stone-ground yellow cornmeal (chilled)

1 tablespoon cornstarch

2 tablespoons sugar

1$^1/_2$ teaspoons salt

Prepare the butter and lard, if using. Cut the butter into ½-inch (12-mm) cubes (a bench scraper is perfect for this, but a sharp knife works well too), and cut the lard into small pieces. Return them to the fridge to cool.

In a liquid measuring cup, stir together the milk and vinegar. Refrigerate the mixture until ready to use.

On a clean flat surface or in a large shallow bowl, toss the flour, cornmeal, cornstarch, sugar, and salt together lightly to blend. Add the butter and lard (if using) to the dry ingredients and, using the tool of your choice (see Tools of the Trade, page 20), cut the fat into the flour with speed and patience, until the fat has been reduced to small pea-sized chunks. Try to use a straight up-and-down motion, as the more you press on the flour the more tough gluten will develop. Avoid using your fingers, as the heat from your hands will melt the fat and further encourage gluten development. Unlike with pasta or bread, gluten is the enemy of pie dough, so be gentle, and be quick!

Once your fat has been cut down to size, spread your mixture out to expose as much surface area as possible. Gently drizzle about half of your milk mixture over the flour, trying to cover as wide an area as you can. Using bench scrapers or a large spoon, lightly toss the flour over the liquid, then spread everything out again, and repeat the process with the second half of the liquid.

You should now have a dough that will just hold together when pressed against the bowl, with visible little chunks of butter. If you need to add more liquid to bind it, do so with more cold milk, adding a tablespoon at a time until you reach the right texture. It's not an exact science, as everything from the humidity in the air to the dryness of your flour will affect the consistency of your dough.

Once you've reached your goal, cover the dough tightly in plastic wrap and refrigerate it for at least 1 hour. The dough can be kept in the fridge for up to 1 week, well wrapped, or in the freezer for up to 2 months.

Food Processor Instructions

Prepare the butter, lard, and milk mixture as instructed above.

In the work bowl of a food processor fitted with a metal blade, add the dry ingredients and pulse once to blend. Remove the lid and add the fat. Replace the lid, have your milk mixture ready, and turn on the processor. After a couple of seconds, start to slowly pour the milk down the feed tube of the processor. As soon as all the milk has been added, turn off the machine. Pour the dough onto plastic wrap, bind it tightly, and refrigerate it for at least 1 hour.

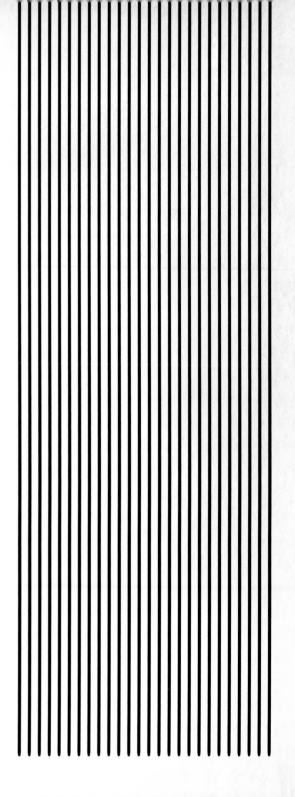

VEGAN PÂTE BRISÉE

This is a dairy-free version of my classic crust, and can be used in its place for most recipes. Just keep in mind that the coconut oil and milk impart their flavor to the crust, so it won't necessarily work for every recipe. Because it lacks dairy, this crust doesn't brown the way a butter crust will, so be careful not to overbake it.

MAKES enough for one double-crust 9-inch (23-cm) pie

12 ounces (340 g/ approximately 3 cups) unbleached all-purpose flour, chilled

2 tablespoons sugar

1¹/₂ teaspoons salt

1 cup (225 ml) virgin coconut oil, chilled and cut into small pieces

¹/₂ cup (120 ml) coconut milk, chilled

On a clean flat surface or in a large shallow bowl, stir together the flour, sugar, and salt. Add the coconut oil and, using the tool of your choice (see Tools of the Trade, page 20), cut the fat into the flour until the mixture resembles coarse meal. Slowly drizzle in the coconut milk in three stages, tossing the mixture after every addition. The dough should just hold together. Increase or decrease the amount of coconut milk as necessary. Cover the dough tightly in plastic wrap and refrigerate it for at least 1 hour. The dough can be kept in the fridge for up to 1 week, well wrapped, or in the freezer for up to 2 months.

Food Processor Instructions

In the work bowl of a food processor fitted with a metal blade, add the dry ingredients and pulse once to blend. Remove the lid and add the coconut oil. Replace the lid, have your coconut milk ready, and turn on the processor. After a couple of seconds, start to slowly pour the milk down the feed tube of the processor. As soon as all the milk has been added, turn off the machine. Pour the dough onto plastic wrap, bind it tightly, and refrigerate it for at least 1 hour.

1/2 cup (120 ml) whole milk	1/4 cup (20 g) high-quality unsweetened cocoa powder
1 tablespoon apple cider vinegar (or any light-colored, mild vinegar)	1/4 cup (50 g) sugar
	1/2 teaspoon salt
12 ounces (340 g/ approximately 3 cups; see Note, page 41) unbleached all-purpose flour (chilled)	3/4 cup (1 1/2 sticks) unsalted European-style cultured butter
	1/4 cup (55 g) rendered leaf lard OR additional butter

In a liquid measuring cup, stir together the vinegar and milk. Refrigerate the mixture until ready to use.

On a clean flat surface or in a large shallow bowl, stir together the flour, cocoa, sugar, and salt. Add the butter and lard (if using) to the dry ingredients and, using the tool of your choice (see Tools of the Trade, page 20), cut the fat into the flour until the mixture has been reduced to small pea-sized chunks. Try to use a straight up-and-down motion, avoiding twisting your wrists, as the more you press on the flour the more tough gluten will develop in the dough. Avoid using your fingers, as the heat from your hands will melt the fat and further encourage gluten development. Unlike with pasta or bread, gluten is the enemy of pie dough, so be gentle, and be quick!

Once your fat has been cut down to size, spread your mixture out gently to expose as much surface area as possible. Gently drizzle about half of your milk mixture over the flour, trying to cover as wide an area as you can. Using bench scrapers or a large spoon, toss the flour over the liquid (don't stir; just lightly toss), then spread everything out again, and repeat the process with the second half of the liquid.

You should now have a dough that will just hold together when pressed against the bowl, with visible little chunks of butter. If you need to add more liquid to bind it, do so with more cold milk, adding a tablespoon at a time until you reach the right texture. It's not an exact science, as everything from the humidity in the air to the dryness of your flour will affect the consistency of your dough.

Once you've reached your goal, cover the dough tightly in plastic wrap and refrigerate it for at least 1 hour. The dough can be kept in the fridge for up to 1 week, well wrapped, or in the freezer for up to 2 months.

CHOCOLATE CRUST

This recipe is not for a chocolate cookie crust; you'll find one of those in the next section. Rather, this is a classic pie crust, but full of rich chocolate flavor. It's similar to the classic pie crust recipe above, and the technique for making it is the same, but it has less salt, more sugar, and a nice scoop of cocoa.

MAKES enough for one double-crust 9-inch (23-cm) pie

Food Processor Instructions

Prepare the butter, lard, and milk mixture as instructed above.

In the work bowl of a food processor fitted with a metal blade, add the dry ingredients and pulse once to blend. Remove the lid and add the fat. Replace the lid, have your milk mixture ready, and turn on the processor. After a couple of seconds, start to slowly pour the milk down the feed tube of the processor. As soon as all the milk has been added, turn off the machine. Pour the dough onto plastic wrap, bind it tightly, and refrigerate it for at least 1 hour.

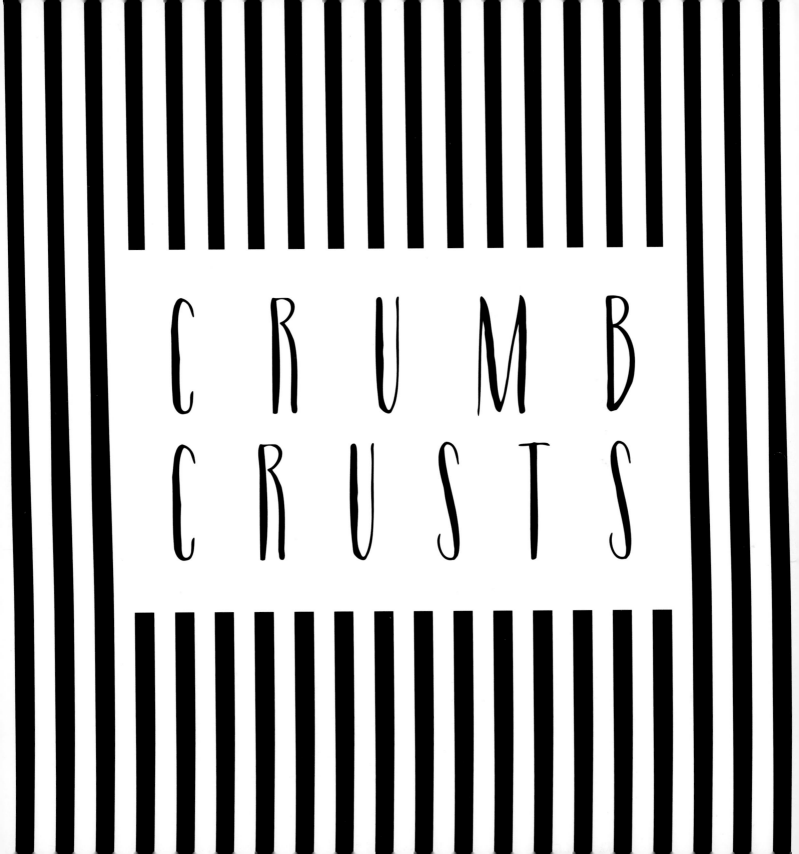

CRUMB
CRUSTS

Crumb crusts are those in which cookies (or crackers, biscuits, pretzels . . .) are crushed into small crumbs, mixed with melted butter, and pressed into a pie plate. These are usually used for custard, pudding, and icebox pies. The amount of fat used depends upon the texture of the crumbs: drier crumbs need more, whereas richer cookies such as shortbread require less.

With the exception of pretzels, saltines, and English digestive biscuits, I bake all of the cookies for my crumb crusts from scratch. It adds a good deal more time and labor, but I like to know exactly what's going into my pies. If you opt for premade cookies and crackers, go for all-natural and organic options.

For those of you who suffer from wheat allergies or celiac disease, I've included a recipe for a gluten-free flour blend (see page 51) that you can substitute for the flour in these cookie recipes. I have tried time and again to develop a gluten-free dough-based crust that I'm happy with, but, unfortunately, I haven't found a recipe that satisfies my flavor criteria.

Most recipes for crumb crusts call for adding additional sugar to the mixture. I eschew this in my recipes since I like a more savory crust, and generally find the extra sugar unnecessary.

technique

The technique for constructing a crumb crust is fairly simple, but there are a few methods that will yield the best results. A food processor is very useful for this. You fill the bowl with enough cookies for about 1½ cups (175 g) of crumbs, process them until fine, and then drizzle in melted butter until they have the consistency of wet sand and just hold together when squeezed. If you don't have a food processor, take a rolling pin and run it over a sealed plastic bag of cookies. You can also get some aggression out by bashing stubborn chunks with the rolling pin—it's very cathartic. Then just stir in the butter in a mixing bowl.

Once you have the right mixture of crumbs and butter, pile about 1 cup (115 g) of crumbs into your pie plate. I like to start with the sides, using the flat top surface of the index and middle fingers of my writing hand to press the crumbs firmly against the walls of my pie dish. I use the index finger of my other hand to form a sort of barrier to prevent the crumbs from loosely spilling over the edge of the dish. This gives a nicely uniform, clean line of crust. When the sides are complete, fill the bottom with more crumbs and press down firmly with your fingers or the bottom of a measuring cup. Make sure you don't have an excess of crumbs built up in the bottom corner; you want an even thickness throughout.

blind-baking

The process of blind-baking crumb crusts is much simpler than with dough-based crusts. Because you're dealing with cookies that have already been baked once, you don't need to worry as much about your crust shrinking or slumping, and you don't need to line the crust with foil or weights.

To blind-bake any crumb crust, preheat the oven to 350°F (175°C). Assemble your crust as directed above, and let it chill in the freezer or fridge until firm. Bake for 10 minutes, remove it from the oven, and allow it to cool completely.

GLUTEN-FREE FLOUR BLEND

For my gluten-intolerant and celiac-suffering friends, I'm including this flour blend, which you can use instead of all-purpose flour in the cookie recipes in this chapter. I'm not happy with the results in my dough-based crusts, unfortunately, but in cookie crusts it works wonderfully.

These ingredients are much more prevalent nowadays, and should be easy to find at health food stores and online.

For every 4 ounces (115 g/approximately 1 cup) of all-purpose flour, substitute this following blend of gluten-free flours.

1¼ ounces (35 g) white rice flour

1¼ ounces (35 g) tapioca flour

¾ ounce (20 g) brown rice flour

¾ ounce (20 g) millet flour

Make your life easy: Mix together a big batch of this flour blend and keep it stored in an airtight container.

VANILLA WAFER CRUST

We all know **vanilla wafers** from **that classic American dessert, banana pudding.** They make **wonderful layers for icebox cakes, but you can also use them for pie crusts with delicious results. They're a must for my Creamsicle Chiffon Pie (page 166).**

VANILLA WAFER COOKIES

MAKES approximately three dozen cookies

$^1/_2$ cup (1 stick/115 g) unsalted butter, at room temperature

$^3/_4$ cup (150 g) sugar

1 large egg

1 tablespoon vanilla extract

8 ounces (225 g/ approximately 2 cups) unbleached all-purpose flour

1 teaspoon baking powder

$^1/_4$ teaspoon salt

Preheat the oven to 350°F (175°C). Line two baking sheets with Silpats or parchment.

In a stand mixer fitted with the paddle attachment or in a large bowl, beat together the butter and sugar on low speed until they are light and fluffy. Beat in the egg and vanilla. In a separate bowl, combine the flour, baking powder, and salt, add them to the wet ingredients, and mix until fully blended.

Roll teaspoon-size balls of dough between your palms, flatten them slightly with your fingertips, and arrange them 2 inches (5 cm) apart on your baking sheets. Alternatively, you can chill the dough overnight or for up to 1 week, then roll it out on a lightly floured surface to 1 inch (2.5 cm) thick, and use a 2-inch (5-cm) cookie cutter.

Bake the cookies for 12 to 15 minutes, rotating the pan once halfway through, until the edges are golden brown. Remove them to a wire rack to cool completely. The cookies can be stored in an airtight container for up to 10 days. The dough can be frozen for up to 2 months.

VANILLA WAFER CRUST

MAKES one 9-inch (23-cm) pie crust

1 1/2 cups (175 g) finely ground vanilla wafer crumbs

5 to 8 tablespoons (70 to 115 g) unsalted butter, melted

Preheat the oven to 350°F (175°C).

Crumble the cookies into the work bowl of a food processor and process until finely ground. Alternatively, you can put them in a bag and whack them with a rolling pin until finely crushed. Pour the butter into the crumbs and mix (hands are best for this) until the butter is fully incorporated and the texture is that of wet sand. Firmly press the crumbs against the sides of a 9-inch (23-cm) pie pan, then against the bottom of the pan (the underside of a measuring cup works well for smoothing the bottom crust). Chill the crust for at least 15 minutes to help prevent it from crumbling when serving.

Bake the crust for 10 minutes, or until golden. Remove it and allow it to cool before filling.

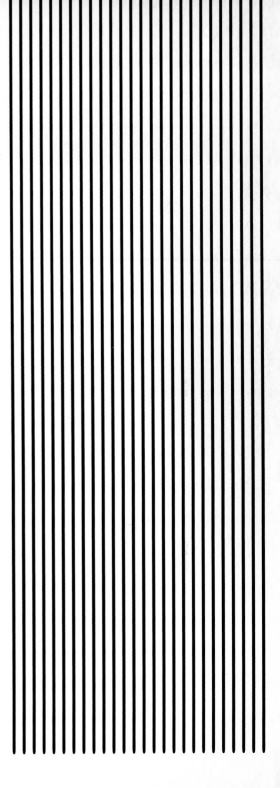

GRAHAM CRACKER CRUST

This crust is essential for my S'mores Pie (page 130), and a perfect counterpart to the tart, creamy filling of my Key Lime Pie (page 182). You're sure to find many uses for this sweet, versatile cracker. The recipe makes more crackers than you'll need. Save the rest, or make some s'mores!

GRAHAM CRACKERS

MAKES 12 to 15 large graham crackers

1/2 cup (100 g) firmly packed dark brown sugar

1/4 cup (1/2 stick/60 g) unsalted butter, at room temperature

3 tablespoons clover honey

3 tablespoons whole milk

1 tablespoon vanilla extract

4 ounces (115 g/approximately 1 cup) unbleached all-purpose flour, plus extra for rolling

2 ounces (60 g/approximately 1/2 cup) graham flour (or whole wheat or all-purpose)

1/2 teaspoon baking soda

1/4 teaspoon cinnamon

1/4 teaspoon salt

In a large bowl or stand mixer, cream together the sugar and butter until light and fluffy. Beat in the honey, milk, and vanilla until blended. In a medium bowl whisk together the flours, baking soda, cinnamon, and salt until combined. Add the dry ingredients to the wet ingredients and beat until just combined. Turn the dough out onto a sheet of plastic wrap, seal tightly, and refrigerate for about 2 hours or overnight.

Preheat the oven to 350°F (175°C).

Divide the dough in half. Sift an even layer of flour onto the work surface and roll half of the dough into a long rectangle about ⅛ inch (3 mm) thick. The dough will be sticky; flour as necessary. Using a wheel cutter or paring knife, cut the dough into 6 to 8 even rectangles. Transfer them to a Silpat or parchment-lined baking sheet. Repeat with the second half of the dough.

Bake the crackers for 25 minutes, until golden brown and slightly firm to the touch, rotating the sheets halfway through to ensure even baking. Allow them to cool. The crackers can be stored in an airtight container for up to one week.

GRAHAM CRACKER CRUST

MAKES one 9-inch (23-cm) pie crust

1¹/₂ cups (175 g) finely ground
   graham cracker crumbs

5 to 8 tablespoons (70 to
   115 g) unsalted butter,
   melted

Preheat the oven to 350°F (175°C).

Crumble the graham crackers into the work bowl of a food processor and process until finely ground. Alternatively, you can put them in a bag and whack them with a rolling pin until finely crushed. Pour the butter into the crumbs and mix (hands are best for this) until the butter is fully incorporated and the texture is that of wet sand. Firmly press the crumbs against the sides of a 9-inch (23-cm) pie pan, then against the bottom of the pan (the underside of a measuring cup works well for smoothing the bottom crust). Chill the crust for at least 15 minutes to help prevent it from crumbling when serving.

Bake the crust for 10 minutes, or until lightly browned. Remove it and allow it to cool before filling.

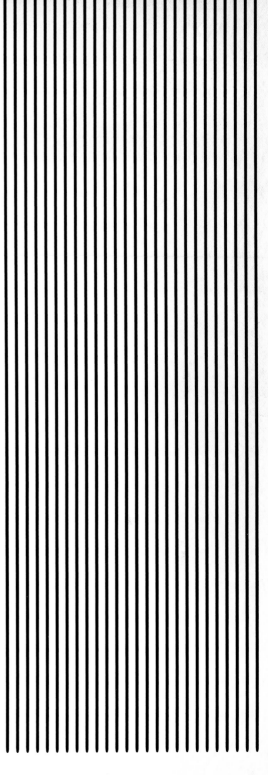

GINGERSNAP CRUST

This recipe is a must-have for my Mexican Chocolate Pie (page 194) and puts an interesting spin on classics like Pumpkin Spice (page 172). Use it whenever you want a slightly spicy, warm accent to your dessert. This makes more cookies than you'll need for one crust, but I'm sure you'll find a use for the rest.

GINGERSNAP COOKIES

MAKES   approximately two dozen cookies

8 ounces (225 g/ approximately 2 cups) unbleached all-purpose flour	$^1/_2$ teaspoon salt
1 tablespoon ground ginger	1 cup (200 g) firmly packed dark brown sugar
$1^1/_2$ teaspoons baking soda	$^1/_2$ cup (1 stick/115 g) unsalted butter, at room temperature
$^1/_2$ teaspoon ground allspice	$^1/_2$ cup (118 ml) molasses
$^1/_2$ teaspoon ground cloves	1 large egg, at room temperature

Preheat the oven to 350°F (175°C). Line two baking sheets with Silpats or parchment.

In a medium mixing bowl, whisk together the flour, ginger, baking soda, allspice, cloves, and salt.

In the bowl of a stand mixer fitted with the paddle attachment, beat together the sugar and butter on low speed until they are light and fluffy, 1 to 2 minutes, or cream together in a bowl with a hand mixer or wooden spoon. Add the molasses and egg and beat on medium for 1 minute. Add the dry ingredients to the wet and stir until well combined.

With a tablespoon, drop the dough onto the baking sheets approximately 2 inches (5 cm) apart. (Alternatively, you can chill the dough overnight and roll it out on a well-floured surface, cutting it with a 2-inch/5-cm cookie cutter.)

Bake the cookies on the middle rack of the oven for 12 to 15 minutes, rotating the pan once halfway through, until brown around the edges.

Remove the cookies from the oven and allow them to cool on the baking sheets for 1 minute before transferring them to a rack to cool completely. Store them in an airtight container for up to 1 week. The dough can be frozen for up to 2 months.

GINGERSNAP CRUST

MAKES one 9-inch (23-cm) pie crust

1¹/₂ cups (175 g) finely ground
    gingersnap crumbs

5 to 8 tablespoons (70 to
    115 g) unsalted butter,
    melted

Preheat the oven to 350°F (175°C).

Crumble the gingersnaps into the work bowl of a food processor and process until finely ground. Alternatively, you can put them in a bag and whack them with a rolling pin until finely crushed. Pour the butter into the crumbs and mix (hands are best for this) until the butter is fully incorporated and the texture is that of wet sand. Firmly press the crumbs against the sides of a 9-inch (23-cm) pie pan, then against the bottom of the pan (the underside of a measuring cup works well for smoothing the bottom crust). Chill the crust for at least 15 minutes to help prevent it from crumbling when serving.

Bake the crust for 10 minutes, or until slightly darkened and fragrant. Remove it and allow it to cool before filling.

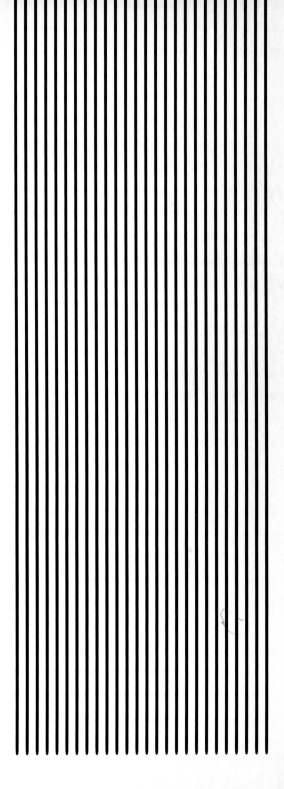

CHOCOLATE COOKIE CRUST

This crust is great for anything wanting a rich cocoa edge. I use it for my Raspberry Vinegar Tart (page 120), and I love it with Samantha Bee's Salty Caramel Pie (page 70) as well. The cookie recipe yields more than you need for a single crust, but I suspect you'll find something to do with the extras.

CHOCOLATE COOKIES

MAKES approximately two dozen cookies

6 ounces (170 g/approximately 1½ cups) unbleached all-purpose flour	½ cup maple syrup
3 ounces (85 g/approximately ¾ cup) high-quality unsweetened cocoa powder	1 large egg
	1 teaspoon vanilla extract
½ teaspoon baking soda	¾ cup (1½ sticks/170 g) unsalted butter, at room temperature
½ teaspoon salt	½ cup (110 g) firmly packed dark brown sugar

In a large bowl, whisk together the flour, cocoa, baking soda, and salt to blend. In a separate bowl, stir together the syrup, egg, and vanilla. In the bowl of a stand mixer fitted with the paddle attachment or in a large mixing bowl, beat together the butter and sugar on low speed until they are light and fluffy. Pour in the liquid ingredients and mix until fully blended. Add the dry ingredients and mix until just combined. Use a spatula to give it a final stir, scraping down the sides and ensuring the flour is incorporated.

Chill the dough in the refrigerator for at least 30 minutes or overnight.

Preheat the oven to 350°F (175°C). Line two baking sheets with Silpats or parchment.

Take spoonfuls of dough and roll them into balls about 1½ inches (4 cm) in diameter. Put 8 on each sheet, about 2 inches (5 cm) apart, and press them down gently to flatten into disks. Repeat with the remaining dough.

Bake the cookies for about 10 minutes, rotating the pans halfway through, until puffy. Remove the cookies and allow them to cool completely. The cookies can be stored at room temperature in an airtight container for up to one week.

CHOCOLATE COOKIE CRUST

MAKES one 9-inch (23-cm) pie crust

1¹/₂ cups (175 g) finely ground chocolate cookie crumbs

5 to 8 tablespoons (70 to 115 g) unsalted butter, melted

Preheat the oven to 350°F (175°C).

Crumble the cookies into the work bowl of a food processor and process until finely ground. Alternatively, you can put them in a bag and whack them with a rolling pin until finely crushed. Pour the butter into the crumbs and mix (hands are best for this) until the butter is fully incorporated and the texture is that of wet sand. Firmly press the crumbs against the sides of a 9-inch (23-cm) pie pan, then against the bottom of the pan (the underside of a measuring cup works well for smoothing the bottom crust). Chill the crust for at least 15 minutes to help prevent it from crumbling when serving.

Bake the crust for 10 minutes, or until fragrant. Remove it and allow it to cool before filling.

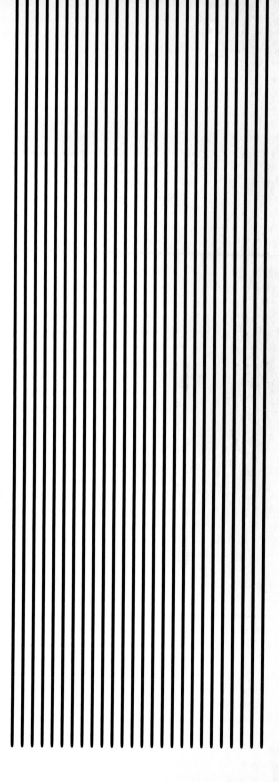

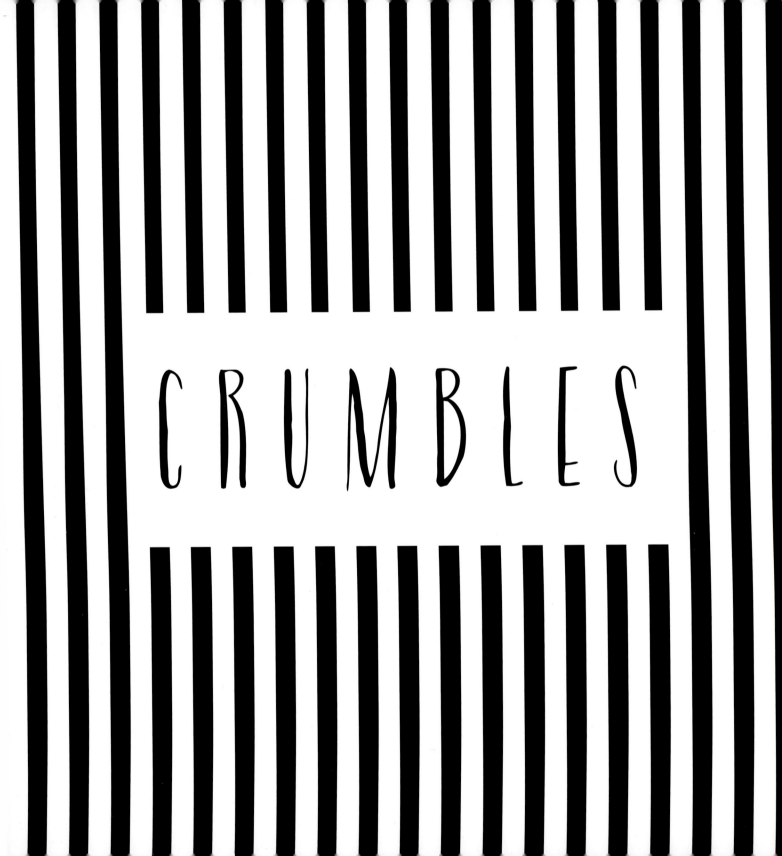

From time to time I like to skip the top crust and sprinkle a sweet, streusely, crumbly mixture of buttery sugary goodness on my pie. Crumble toppings are very traditional, very rustic, and very delicious. You can substitute them for the top crusts in a number of pies in this book, such as the Sour Cherry (page 124) or the Blueberry-Nectarine Pie (page 105).

I'm providing you with my standard crumble recipe, but keep in mind that this is very versatile and can be adapted with whatever you want to toss in. Don't like oats? Use flour. Out of almonds? Throw in some pecans instead. Allergic to nuts? Skip 'em! It's hard to mess this one up.

1 cup (155 g) rolled oats (not instant)

1/2 cup (110 g) firmly packed dark brown sugar

1/4 cup (30 g) unbleached all-purpose flour

1/4 cup (35 g) toasted almonds, chopped

1/4 teaspoon salt

1/4 teaspoon cinnamon

1/2 cup (1 stick/115 g) unsalted butter, cut into pieces, at room temperature

In a large mixing bowl, stir together all the ingredients but the butter. Using your fingers, rub the butter into the dry ingredients until it's loosely combined and forms large crumbs. Sprinkle the crumble mixture over your pie filling and bake as directed.

MAKES enough to cover one 9-inch (23-cm) pie

BAKING
WITH THE
SEASONS

There's a lot of talk these days about eating local foods, organic growing practices, and maintaining a low carbon footprint by eating produce when it's in season. The origins of pie making are rooted in this approach to food, for it adapts to, and embraces, whatever happens to be in season. During lean times, you need look no further than your pantry to whip up a modest chess pie, which is simply a custard made with just a few humble ingredients. When crops are more abundant, pies are the perfect showcase for just-picked, sun-ripened fruit.

The recipes in this book follow the changing seasons, and I encourage you to do the same. December strawberries taste like potatoes. Cans of pumpkin just don't seem appealing in the heat of July. When you wait for an entire year to eat a ripe cherry, it's the best cherry you've ever tasted. All politics aside, seasonal ingredients just taste better, which means your pies will taste better too.

March

Here in New York, it takes a while before
it really starts to feel like spring. In
March, I'm still dipping into my arsenal
of winter standbys: citrus and tropical
fruits, nuts, chocolate, and custards.

███████████████████████████████████

SAMOA 66

PINEAPPLE 69

SAMANTHA BEE'S SALTY
CARAMEL 70

LEMON CREAM 72

SESAME-HONEY 73

CHOCOLATE-LAVENDER
TEATIME 74

SHORTBREAD CRUST

1¹/₂ cups (156 g) shortbread cookie crumbs, from 15 to 20 cookies

2 to 4 tablespoons (30 to 55 g) unsalted butter, melted

FILLING

2 cups (400 g) sugar

¹/₄ cup (60 ml) corn syrup

¹/₂ cup (1 stick/115 g) unsalted butter

1 (14-ounce/414-ml) can full-fat coconut milk, refrigerated (organic preferred)

1 teaspoon vanilla extract

¹/₄ teaspoon salt

1 cup (113 g) toasted shredded coconut (organic preferred)

TOPPING

¹/₄ cup (28 g) toasted shredded coconut (organic preferred)

4 ounces (115 g) semisweet chocolate, chopped or chips

¹/₄ cup (60 ml) heavy cream

Make the crust: Grind the cookies in a food processor until finely ground or seal them in a plastic bag and crush them with a rolling pin. Pour in the butter (they're very buttery already, so use just a little at a time) and mix (hands are best for this) until the texture is that of wet sand. Firmly press the crumbs into a 9-inch (23-cm) pie pan (see page 50). Chill the crust in the freezer or fridge while preheating the oven to 350°F (175°C). Bake it for about 10 minutes, until golden, and then let it cool completely.

Make the filling: In a heavy-bottomed saucepan, stir together ½ cup (120 ml) water, the sugar, and corn syrup until the sugar is mostly dissolved. Cook over medium-high heat, moving the pan around occasionally, until the caramel has turned a dark amber and reached 360°F (180°C) on a candy thermometer. Keep a close eye at this stage, as the caramel can burn very quickly!

RECIPE CONTINUES

SAMOA PIE

I wasn't the greatest Girl Scout. I didn't get all the cool badges, and I don't know much about building fires or constructing canoes, but I was an expert when it came to those cookies. My favorites by far were (and are) the Samoas—full of toasty coconut, gooey caramel, buttery shortbread, and rich chocolate, they are heavenly. (Pro tip: They're even better out of the freezer!) I knew I had to make a pie version of this perfect cookie, so the caramel (my favorite part) could be the star of the show. This is pure nostalgic goodness; no uniform required.

MAKES one 9-inch (23-cm) pie

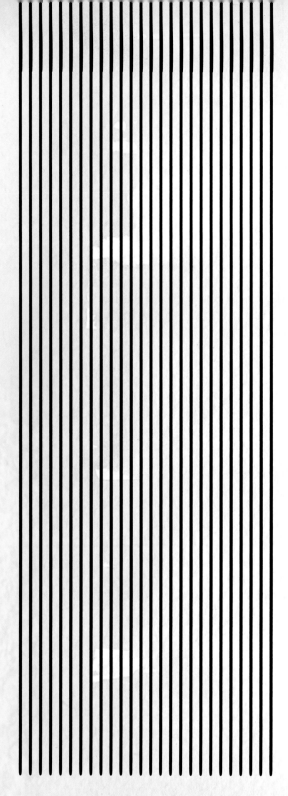

Remove the caramel from the heat and immediately start to whisk in the butter. Be very careful here: The caramel will start to bubble violently and release a lot of hot steam. Open the chilled can of coconut milk, and spoon off the thick white coconut cream from the top, discarding the remaining water. Whisk this coconut cream into the caramel until it is fully dissolved, then add the vanilla and salt. Stir in the toasted coconut, and pour the filling into your prebaked pie shell.

Refrigerate the pie, uncovered, for at least 1 hour, until the surface is set. Sprinkle the toasted coconut over the surface of the pie.

Make the topping: Heat the cream until scalded, and then pour it over the chocolate. Let it sit for a minute, then whisk until glossy. Using a fork, drizzle the ganache over the surface of the pie in a crosshatch pattern, then sprinkle over the toasted coconut. Return the pie, uncovered, to the fridge to fully set, for at least 4 hours but preferably overnight. Serve the pie at room temperature. Running a sharp knife under hot water will make it easier to slice through the sticky caramel filling. This pie can be kept in the refrigerator for up to 1 week, covered in plastic wrap.

FILLING

4 large eggs

1 cup (200 g) sugar

Zest and juice of 1 lime

2 tablespoons dark rum (optional)

1/4 teaspoon salt

1/4 cup (30 g) unbleached all-purpose flour

1/4 cup (1/2 stick/55 g) melted butter

2 cups (362 g) chopped fresh pineapple (from 1 medium-large pineapple)

Classic Pie Crust (page 38) for one double-crust 9-inch (23-cm) pie

Egg wash (page 25) or milk, for glaze

Raw sugar, for garnish

Preheat the oven to 425°F (220°C).

In a large bowl, lightly beat the eggs, then whisk in the sugar, lime zest and juice, rum (if using), and salt. In a separate small bowl, whisk together the flour and butter until fully blended, then whisk them into the egg mixture. Stir in the pineapple.

Roll out one half of the dough into a circle about 11 inches (28 cm) in diameter. Transfer it to a 9-inch (23-cm) pie plate, trim the overhang to 1 inch (2.5 cm), and fill it with the pineapple mixture. Brush the rim of the pie crust with egg wash or milk.

Roll out the remaining circle of dough to about 10 inches (25 cm), lay it over the pie, and trim and crimp the edges to your liking. Cut slits in the top crust, paint it with egg wash or milk, and sprinkle the top with raw sugar.

Bake the pie on a baking sheet for 20 minutes, rotating it once halfway through. Lower the temperature to 350°F (175°C), and bake it for another 30 to 40 minutes, until the crust is nicely browned and fully baked and the filling doesn't jiggle under the crust when the baking sheet is moved. Allow the pie to cool completely before serving. This pie can be kept refrigerated for up to 1 week; allow it to come to room temperature or heat it gently in a warm oven before serving. This pie can also be frozen after baking: Wrap it well in plastic, then in foil, and freeze it for up to 2 months.

PINEAPPLE PIE

Ah, pineapple. My favorite fruit. I eat fresh pineapple almost daily. I just can't get enough, so this recipe was inevitable. Pineapple can be a finicky ingredient because it contains an enzyme that does not get along with most custards and gelatins (they just refuse to set), which is why most pineapple dessert recipes call for canned fruit that has been precooked, neutralizing that pesky enzyme. I love the flavor of the fresh fruit, however, and set about finding a recipe that would work. Here it is—feel free to pair it with coconut sorbet. I think that will make you happy. You can also pair it with Toasted Coconut Cream Pie (see page 92 for a photo of a Pineapple/Toasted Coconut Pie Stack!).

MAKES one 9-inch (23-cm) pie

SAMANTHA BEE'S SALTY CARAMEL PIE

In the fall of 2011, I got a call from *Food & Wine* magazine about doing a profile with some recipes for their big November issue. Obviously, I was elated. That elation turned to freaking-out-stupefaction when I discovered that Samantha Bee (brilliant writer-producer-satirist-and-*Daily-Show*-heroine) was the author, and that she wanted to bake with me. It turns out that in addition to being a comedic superstar, Samantha is a pretty serious home baker. We had a great time, and when she jokingly nudged me to name a pie for her, I took note. It doesn't hurt that she had some flavor ideas right in my wheelhouse: "pretzel crust, something fudgy or caramelly perhaps?" Samantha, your wish is my command.

This recipe calls for brown butter (see Note, page 86), but in a pinch regular butter will do beautifully.

MAKES one 9-inch (23-cm) pie

PRETZEL CRUST

8 ounces (225 g) pretzels (pick your favorite kind)

6 to 8 tablespoons (85 to 115 g) unsalted butter, melted (pretzels can be very dry, so you may need more)

FILLING

1½ cups (300 g) sugar

½ cup (120 ml) honey

½ cup (120 ml) heavy cream

½ cup (1 stick/115 g) brown butter (see Note, page 86)

2 tablespoons mascarpone

1 teaspoon vanilla extract

½ teaspoon sea salt

TOPPING

¼ cup (120 ml) heavy cream

4 ounces (115 g) bittersweet chocolate, chopped

Make the crust: Grind the pretzels in a food processor until finely ground or seal them in a plastic bag and crush them with a rolling pin. Pour in the butter and mix (hands are best for this) until the texture is that of wet sand. You may need more or less butter, depending on the texture of the pretzels. Firmly press the crumbs into a 9-inch (23-cm) pie pan (see page 50). Chill the crust in the freezer or fridge.

Make the filling: In a heavy-bottomed saucepan, stir together ½ cup (120 ml) water, the sugar, and honey until the sugar is mostly dissolved. Cook over medium-high heat, moving the pan around occasionally, until the caramel has turned dark amber and reached 340°F (170°C) on a candy thermometer.

Remove the caramel from the heat and slowly pour the cream down the side of the pan, whisking constantly. Be very careful here: The caramel will start to bubble violently and release a lot of hot steam. Whisk in the butter, then the mascarpone, then the vanilla and salt. Pour the filling into your pre-baked pie shell, and refrigerate it, uncovered, until fully set—at least 5 hours.

Make the topping: Heat the cream until scalded, and then pour it over the chocolate. Let it sit for a minute, then whisk until glossy. Spread or drizzle the ganache over the filling, allow it to set, and serve. This pie can be refrigerated for up to 1 week, covered well in plastic wrap. Allow it to come to room temperature before serving. For easier slicing, run your knife under hot water first to prevent the caramel from sticking to the blade.

LEMON CREAM PIE

This pie was a big hit when they started serving it at Fatty 'Cue, the Southeast Asian—style restaurant in Brooklyn where my brother, Corwin, used to be a chef. I didn't expect something so simple to make such a big splash, but at the end of a rich, fatty meal, nothing hits the spot like the bracing tartness of the fresh lemon juice in this pie. Take the time to squeeze fresh lemons for this one; the bottled stuff just won't do.

MAKES one 9-inch (23-cm) pie

Graham Cracker Crust
(page 54) for one 9-inch
(23-cm) pie

FILLING

1 cup (200 g) sugar

1/4 cup (60 ml) sour cream

4 large eggs

Zest of 1 lemon

1/4 teaspoon salt

3/4 cup (180 ml) freshly
squeezed lemon juice
(from about 4 lemons)

TOPPING

1 cup (240 ml) heavy cream

2 tablespoons sugar

1/2 teaspoon vanilla extract

Preheat the oven to 350°F (175°C). Bake the crust for about 10 minutes, until golden brown. Remove it from the oven and allow it to cool completely while preparing the filling.

Make the filling: In a mixing bowl, whisk together the sugar, sour cream, eggs, lemon zest, and salt until fully blended. Slowly pour in the lemon juice while whisking constantly, until fully incorporated.

Press the crust into a 9-inch (23-cm) pie plate. Put the crust on a baking sheet, fill it with the filling, and bake for 20 to 25 minutes, until the filling has just set and is still slightly wobbly in the center. Remove the pie and allow it to cool completely, at least 1 hour.

Make the topping: In a stand mixer, with a hand mixer, or by hand with a whisk, whip the cream, sugar, and vanilla together until stiff peaks form. Pile the whipped cream on top of the cooled pie, and serve.

This pie can be made ahead, without the topping, and refrigerated for up to 1 week, covered in plastic wrap. Add the topping just before serving.

Classic Pie Crust (page 38) for one 9-inch (23-cm) pie

FILLING

1 cup (240 ml) honey (orange blossom is great with this recipe)

4 large eggs

1/2 cup (60 g) roasted tahini

1 teaspoon vanilla extract

1/4 teaspoon salt

1/4 teaspoon cinnamon

1/2 cup (60 g) untoasted white sesame seeds

Preheat the oven to 425°F (220°C). Roll out the dough into a circle about 11 inches (28 cm) in diameter. Transfer it to a 9-inch (23-cm) pie plate. Blind-bake the pie crust until partially baked (see page 35); set it aside to cool. Lower the oven to 350°F (175°C).

Make the filling: In a large bowl, whisk together the honey, eggs, tahini, vanilla, salt, and cinnamon until fully blended. Stir in the sesame seeds.

Put the crust on a baking sheet. Pour the filling into the crust and bake for 20 to 25 minutes, until the filling has just set and is still slightly wobbly in the center. Remove the pie to cool completely before serving. This pie can be refrigerated for up to 1 week, wrapped well in plastic. Allow it to come to room temperature before serving.

SESAME–HONEY PIE

I've always been a fan of those little sesame candies you can get at various delis, bodegas, and groceries around New York. Wrapped up in cellophane, they are crunchy, nutty, and sweet with the flavor of honey. As is my wont, I decided to transform these tasty morsels into a pie. This is for serious sesame fans!

MAKES one 9-inch (23-cm) pie

Chocolate Cookie (page 58)
or Chocolate Pie Crust
(page 47) for one 9-inch
(23-cm) pie

FILLING

1 cup (240 ml) heavy cream

2 tablespoons Earl Grey tea
leaves (about 2 tea bags)

8 ounces (225 g) bittersweet
chocolate, chopped or
chips

1 large egg, at room
temperature

Zest of 1 lemon

$1/4$ teaspoon salt

TOPPING

1 cup (240 ml) heavy cream

2 tablespoons powdered sugar

2 tablespoons ground
lavender (see Note)

CHOCOLATE LAVENDER TEATIME PIE

For the **Chocolate Cookie Crust,** preheat the oven to 350°F (175°C), and press the crust into a 9-inch (23-cm) pie plate. Bake it for 10 minutes, then let it cool completely. For the **Chocolate Pie Crust**, preheat the oven to 425°F (220°C). Roll out the dough into a circle about 11 inches (28 cm) in diameter. Transfer it to a 9-inch (23-cm) pie plate, trim the overhang to 1 inch (2.5 cm), roll the overhang under, and crimp. Blind-bake the pie crust until partially baked (see page 35); set it aside to cool. Lower the oven to 350°F (175°C).

Make the filling: In a saucepan, heat the cream and tea leaves over medium heat until scalded. Remove it from the heat and allow the tea to steep for about 15 minutes. Remove the tea bags or strain out the tea, and return the infused cream to the pan. Reheat the cream until it is scalded again, and then pour it over the chocolate in a heatproof bowl. Allow the mixture to stand for 1 to 2 minutes, then whisk everything together until fully blended into a smooth ganache. Whisk in the egg, zest, and salt.

Put the crust on a baking sheet. Pour the filling into the crust and bake for 20 to 25 minutes, until the filling has just set and is still slightly wobbly in the center. Remove the pie to cool completely.

Make the topping: In a stand mixer, with a hand mixer, or by hand with a whisk, whip the cream, sugar, and lavender together until soft peaks form. Spread or pipe the whipped cream over the cooled pie and serve. The crust and filling can be baked up to 1 week ahead. Just cover well in plastic wrap and refrigerate, then make the topping just before serving.

NOTE It's important to use dried culinary (unsprayed) lavender in this recipe, not an extract. If you can only find extract, skip it entirely. Grind the lavender in a spice grinder or coffee mill so it disperses finely throughout the whipped cream topping.

This pie was inspired by Keavy, my partner in Butter & Scotch. She is absolutely virtuosic when it comes to using lavender, which so often in desserts is either barely discernible or total overkill (soap, anyone?). Her chocolate-lavender cupcakes blew my mind when I first tasted them, and I knew I could make a killer pie with the same flavors. I've added a nice hit of Earl Grey tea to this one as well, which is a natural pairing for dark chocolate and complements the floral, herbaceous flavor of the lavender.

MAKES   one 9-inch (23-cm) pie

April

In early spring, we're waiting for the berries and stone fruits of summer, but we've still got beautiful winter citrus to work with, and our old friends chocolate, nuts, and caramel. The most exciting crop for me, and the one that marks spring's true beginning, is rhubarb.

'''''''''''''''''''''''''''''''''''

RHUBARB FRANGIPANE 78

CHAI CHESS 80

AVOCADO CREAM 82

SHOO-FLY 84

SMOKED ALMOND 87

RHUBARB FRANGIPANE PIE

For some, the beginning of spring is marked by budding crocuses and blooming daffodils. For me, it's all about the rhubarb. After a long winter of baking endless nut, citrus, and chocolate cream pies, the emergence of those leafy pink stalks from the ground is a harbinger of the coming bounty of spring and summer fruits. Some wait until strawberries are in season a few weeks later to start baking with rhubarb, but I use it as soon as humanly possible. Toasted almond frangipane is a lovely, creamy foil to the tartness of the rhubarb, and adds an extra layer of flavor without overwhelming the star ingredient.

MAKES one 9-inch (23-cm) pie

Classic Pie (page 38) or Cornmeal Crust (page 44) for one double-crust 9-inch (23-cm) pie

FRANGIPANE FILLING
- ²⁄₃ cup (75 g) slivered almonds, toasted
- ¹⁄₃ cup (65 g) sugar
- 6 tablespoons (³⁄₄ stick/85 g) unsalted butter, at room temperature
- 1 large egg
- 1 tablespoon unbleached all-purpose flour
- 1/4 teaspoon vanilla extract

RHUBARB FILLING
- ³⁄₄ cup (150 g) sugar
- 3 tablespoons cornstarch
- ¹⁄₄ teaspoon salt
- 1¹⁄₂ pounds (680 g) fresh rhubarb, chopped into 1-inch (2.5-cm) pieces (about 3 cups; remove any tough strings)
- Zest of 1 orange
- Egg wash (page 25) or milk, for glaze
- Raw sugar, for garnish

Preheat the oven to 425°F (220°C). On a lightly floured surface, roll out half of the dough into an 11-inch (28-cm) circle about ⅛ to ¼ inch (3 to 6 mm) thick. Line a 9-inch (23-cm) pie plate with the dough, and trim the overhang to 1 inch (2.5 cm). Refrigerate the crust until ready to bake.

Make the frangipane filling: In a food processor, grind the almonds and sugar until they are sandy. Add the butter, then the egg, flour, and vanilla and mix until smooth.

Make the rhubarb filling: In a large bowl, mix together the sugar, cornstarch, and salt. Add the rhubarb and orange zest and toss to coat.

Spread the frangipane over the bottom crust. Pile the rhubarb filling on top. Brush the pie shell edges with egg wash or milk.

Roll out the other half of the pie crust into an 11-inch (28-cm) circle. Lay the dough over the surface of the pie. Trim the edges and tuck the dough inward or outward, pressing and rolling the bottom and top crust edges together. Crimp them into a decorative edge, brush with egg wash or milk, and sprinkle raw sugar over the top. Cut vents into the top crust to allow steam to escape.

Put the pie on a baking sheet and bake for 20 minutes, rotating once halfway through. Lower the temperature to 350°F (175°C) and bake for 30 to 40 minutes more, until the crust is golden and the filling is set (you'll see thick juices bubbling out when it's ready). Remove the pie to cool completely on a wire rack, at least 1 hour.

This pie can be refrigerated for up to 1 week, covered in plastic wrap. Let it come to room temperature before serving, or warm it in a low oven. It can be kept frozen for up to 2 months: Cover it in plastic wrap, then in foil, and let it come to room temperature before serving.

Classic Pie (page 38) or
    Chocolate Pie Crust (page 47)
    for one 9-inch (23-cm) pie

FILLING

4 large eggs

$^3/_4$ cup (150 g) sugar

$^1/_4$ cup (36 g) chai tea
    mixture, ground in a
    spice mill or coffee
    grinder until fine

2 tablespoons unbleached
    all-purpose flour

2 tablespoons unsalted
    butter, melted

$^1/_4$ teaspoon salt

TOPPING

Whipped cream and sliced
    candied ginger
    (optional)

Preheat the oven to 350°F (175°C). Roll out the dough into a circle about 11 inches (28 cm) in diameter. Transfer it to a 9-inch (23-cm) pie plate. Blind-bake the pie crust until partially baked (see page 35); set it aside to cool. Leave the oven on.

Make the filling: In a large bowl, whisk the eggs and sugar together until light and fluffy. Whisk in the tea, flour, butter, and salt. Put the par-baked crust on a baking sheet. Pour the filling into the crust and bake for 25 to 30 minutes, until the filling has just set and is still slightly wobbly in the center. Remove the pie to cool completely before serving. This pie can be refrigerated for up to 1 week, covered well in plastic wrap. Add topping, if using, just before serving.

CHAI CHESS PIE

Chai tea has such an aromatic, intense flavor—I just knew it would be great in a pie, and I was right. Chess pies have simple, classic custard fillings that take well to a range of flavor additions, so play around with the format! This filling pairs beautifully with my chocolate pie crust, but if you really want pure chai flavor with no interference, go with my classic crust.

MAKES   one 9-inch (23-cm) pie

AVOCADO CREAM PIE

Before you get all up in arms talking about guacamole and tacos, let me assure you that avocado is a fruit, and it is absolutely delicious in sweet dishes. All around the world, people are tossing avocados into milkshakes and slurping them down with glee. I urge you to overcome any aversion you might have to the idea of avocado desserts and whip up this pie, because it is insanely delicious.

MAKES one 9-inch (23-cm) pie

Graham Cracker (page 54) or Chocolate Cookie Crust (page 58) for one 9-inch (23-cm) pie

FILLING

4 medium Hass avocados, fully ripe

8 ounces (225 g) cream cheese, at room temperature

1 (14-ounce/400-g) can sweetened condensed milk (organic preferred; get one that's only milk and sugar if possible)

$1/2$ cup (120 ml) fresh lime juice

$1/4$ teaspoon salt

TOPPING

1 cup (240 ml) heavy cream

2 tablespoons powdered sugar

1 teaspoon vanilla extract

Preheat the oven to 350°F (175°C). Pat the crust into a 9-inch (23-cm) pie plate. Bake it for 10 minutes, then let it cool completely.

Make the filling: Halve and pit the avocados; scoop out the flesh into the bowl of a stand mixer or large bowl. Beat the avocado with the cream cheese until smooth. Add in the milk, juice, and salt and beat until fluffy (this can all be done in a blender as well).

Pour the filling into the cooled crust, cover with plastic wrap (allow the plastic to touch the surface of the filling), and refrigerate it until the filling is fully set, at least 4 hours.

Make the topping: In a stand mixer, with a hand mixer, or by hand with a whisk, whip the cream with the sugar and vanilla until stiff peaks form. Pipe or spread the whipped cream over the pie filling. Slice and serve. This pie needs to be served the day it is made, as the avocado filling will oxidize and turn brown if exposed to air for too long.

THE CAKE IS ALL
BUT THE SHOOFLY IS YET
SHE'S CHUST SO WONDERFUL NICE

Classic Pie Crust (page 38) for one 9-inch (23-cm) pie

SYRUP FILLING

1 large egg

1/4 cup (60 ml) unsulphured molasses

1/4 cup (60 ml) maple syrup (Grade B preferred)

1 teaspoon vanilla extract

1/4 teaspoon salt

1/4 teaspoon cinnamon

1/4 teaspoon ground ginger

1/8 teaspoon ground cloves

1/8 teaspoon ground allspice

1/8 teaspoon freshly grated nutmeg

1 cup (240 ml) boiling water

1 teaspoon baking soda

CRUMB FILLING

4 ounces (approximately 1 cup/130 g) unbleached all-purpose flour

1 cup (220 g) firmly packed dark brown sugar

1/4 teaspoon salt

1/4 teaspoon cinnamon

1/4 teaspoon ground ginger

1/8 teaspoon ground cloves

1/8 teaspoon ground allspice

1/8 teaspoon freshly grated nutmeg

1/2 cup (1 stick/115 g) brown butter (see Note), at room temperature

Preheat the oven to 350°F (175°C). Roll out the dough into a circle about 11 inches (28 cm) in diameter. Transfer it to a 9-inch (23-cm) pie plate. Blind-bake the pie crust until partially baked (see page 35); set it aside to cool. Leave the oven on.

Make the syrup filling: In a large bowl, lightly whisk the egg, then whisk in the molasses and syrup. Whisk in the vanilla, salt, and spices. Whisk ¾ cup (180 ml) of the boiling water into your mixture. Stir the baking soda into the remaining ¼ cup (60 ml) remaining water (to make sure the soda is fresh; if it doesn't bubble, you need new soda), and whisk it into the syrup mixture.

Make the crumb filling: In a separate bowl, stir together the flour, sugar, salt, and spices until combined. With your fingers, press the butter into the dry ingredients to form a crumbly mixture.

RECIPE CONTINUES

SHOO-FLY PIE

Shoo-fly pie is popular in Pennsylvania, as a staple of Amish cuisine, and in the South, where it is part of a pantheon of chess pies. The etymology of the name "shoo-fly" has been hotly debated. Some say that due to the sweetness of the pie, and its history as a "cupboard pie" that was left to sit out at room temperature, it was a natural attraction for buzzing flies. Others argue that "shoo-fly" arose out of a mispronunciation of the French word "soufflé," which could be used to describe the light, puffy texture of the custard. I choose no sides: Both interpretations make me happy.

My version is less sweet and more flavorful than most, thanks to maple syrup, brown butter, and a bevy of spices. Somewhere between a pie and a coffee cake, this is a warming, comforting pie that pairs perfectly with a hot cup of joe.

MAKES one 9-inch (23-cm) pie

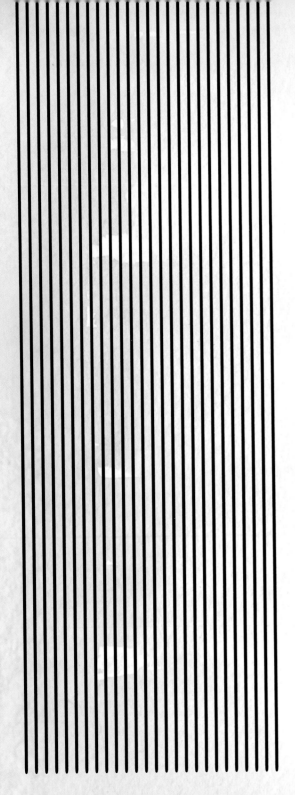

Put the crust on a baking sheet. Pour the syrup into the pie shell. Add in most of the crumble mixture, reserving ¼ to ½ cup (30 to 55 g). Bake the pie for about 20 minutes, then sprinkle the remaining crumble mixture over the top. Bake the pie for another 10 to 20 minutes, until the filling has set. Remove the pie to cool to room temperature or just slightly warm before serving.

NOTE Brown butter, known to the French as *beurre noisette*, takes all the richness of butter and gives it a nutty, toasty aroma. It's easy as pie to make it: Just heat butter in a small heavy-bottomed saucepan over medium heat, whisking occasionally. Keep an eye on it—the butter will foam, then the foam will dissipate and you'll start to see small, light-brown flecks appearing on the bottom of the pan. Use your nose: The butter will start to have a nutty aroma. Once you've got that delicious smell going, remove the pan from the heat to a cool, heatproof surface to stop the cooking (it's easy to go from brown to burnt!). Allow the butter to cool to room temperature before using it in this recipe. You can also store it in an airtight container in the fridge, and use it in all kinds of baking recipes!

Classic Pie (page 38),
    Chocolate Pie (page 47),
    or Chocolate Cookie Crust
    (page 58) for one 9-inch
    (23-cm) pie

FILLING

³/₄ cup (180 ml) heavy cream

1 bag (about 1 tablespoon)
    smoked oolong tea leaves

¹/₂ cup (80 g) smoked almonds

¹/₄ teaspoon salt

4 ounces (115 g) cream
    cheese, at room
    temperature

¹/₂ cup (50 g) powdered sugar

TOPPING

¹/₂ cup (55 g) chopped smoked
    almonds

SMOKED ALMOND PIE

For the **Classic or Chocolate Pie Crusts**, preheat the oven to 425°F (220°C). Roll out the dough into a circle about 11 inches (28 cm) in diameter. Transfer it to a 9-inch (23-cm) pie plate, trim the overhang to about 1 inch (2.5 cm), roll the overhang under, and crimp decoratively. Blind-bake the pie crust until fully baked (see page 35); set it aside to cool. For the **Chocolate Cookie Crust**, preheat the oven to 350°F (175°C). Pat it into a 9-inch (23-cm) pie plate, bake it for 10 minutes, then let it cool completely.

Make the filling: In a heavy-bottomed saucepan, heat the cream and tea until the cream is scalded. Let the tea steep for 10 minutes, then strain and chill the cream until cold.

In a blender or food processor, process the almonds and salt to almond butter (smooth or chunky, your choice!).

In a stand mixer or large bowl, whip the infused cream until it forms stiff peaks. Return it to the fridge to keep chilled.

With a spatula or the paddle attachment of a stand mixer, blend the cream cheese, almond butter, and powdered sugar until they are completely combined. Beat in the whipped cream until just combined. Spread the filling into the prebaked pie shell and refrigerate it until it is firm, about 1 hour. Garnish the top with the chopped almonds, slice the pie, and serve. This pie can be refrigerated for up to 1 week, covered in plastic wrap.

I've never met a nut I didn't like. I don't need much to make me happy: Just roast it, throw on some salt, and I'm good to go. That said, there's something about smoked almonds that sends me over the moon. I love smoky flavors in desserts, and thought this one up over a handful of smoked almonds at a cocktail party. It's sophisticated, it's delicious, and it's sure to disappear fast.

MAKES one 9-inch (23-cm) pie

May

This is the month when spring really kicks into gear. Finally, the sun is starting to shine, the strawberries are getting a blush of pink, and we're dodging fewer raindrops.

....

BUTTERMILK CHESS 90

STRAWBERRY-RHUBARB 91

TOASTED COCONUT CREAM 92

MINT JULEP CREAM 94

IRISH CAR BOMB CREAM 97

NUTELLA 98

BUTTERMILK CHESS PIE

Did you bake some biscuits, only to find half a quart of buttermilk sitting around the fridge? Make excellent use of it in this super-classic Southern-style chess pie. Nothing could be faster or easier to whip up, and it takes to all kinds of adaptations. Feel free to sprinkle some chopped nuts or fresh berries in the bottom of the crust before pouring in your filling—anything goes!

MAKES one 9-inch (23-cm) pie

Classic Pie Crust (page 38) for one 9-inch (23-cm) pie

FILLING
4 large eggs

1 cup (200 g) sugar

$^1/_2$ cup (120 ml) buttermilk

Zest of 1 lemon

2 tablespoons fine cornmeal or all-purpose flour

2 tablespoons unsalted butter, melted

$^1/_4$ teaspoon salt

Preheat the oven to 425°F (220°C). Roll out the dough into a circle about 11 inches (28 cm) in diameter. Transfer it to a 9-inch (23-cm) pie plate, trim the overhang to about 1 inch (2.5 cm), tuck the overhang under, and crimp decoratively. Blind-bake the pie crust until partially baked (see page 35); set it aside to cool. Lower the oven to 350°F (175°C).

Make the filling: In a large bowl, whisk the eggs and sugar together until light and fluffy. Whisk in the buttermilk, lemon zest, cornmeal or flour, butter, and salt. Put the par-baked crust on a baking sheet. Pour the filling into the crust and bake for 25 to 30 minutes, until the filling has just set and is still slightly wobbly in the center. Remove the pie to cool completely before serving. This pie can be refrigerated for up to 1 week, covered in plastic wrap.

Classic Pie (page 38) or Cornmeal Crust (page 44) for one double-crust 9-inch (23-cm) pie

FILLING

About 1 pound (455 g) rhubarb stems, washed and cut into 1-inch (2.5-cm) pieces (remove any tough strings)

4 cups (608 g) fresh strawberries, hulled and halved (cut large berries into smaller pieces)

1/2 teaspoon vanilla extract

Zest of 1 lemon

1 teaspoon grated peeled fresh ginger (optional)

3/4 cup (150 g) sugar

3 tablespoons cornstarch

1/4 teaspoon salt

Egg wash (page 25) or milk, for glaze

Raw sugar, for garnish

STRAWBERRY-RHUBARB PIE

Does it get more classic than strawberry-rhubarb pie? A harbinger of summer, this pie seduces the palate with its tart, herbal notes. This is a great introduction for the rhubarb novice.

Be sure to use *only* the stalks of the rhubarb, as the leaves are poisonous.

MAKES one 9-inch (23-cm) pie

Preheat the oven to 425°F (220°C). Roll out half of the dough into a circle about 11 inches (28 cm) in diameter. Transfer it to a 9-inch (23-cm) pie plate. Trim the overhang to 1 inch (2.5 cm) and refrigerate the crust.

Make the filling: In a large bowl, toss together the rhubarb, strawberries, vanilla, lemon zest, and ginger (if using). In a separate bowl, mix together the sugar, cornstarch, and salt. Just before adding the filling to the crust, toss the fruit in the dry ingredients. Brush the rim of the bottom crust with egg wash or milk.

Roll out the second half of the dough into a circle about 11 inches (28 cm) in diameter. Lay it over the filled pie. Trim the edges, and tuck the top crust over the rim of the bottom crust to form a tight seal. Crimp the edge into whatever pattern you like. Brush the top crust with egg wash or milk, sprinkle it with the raw sugar, and cut a few slits to allow steam to escape.

Put the pie on a baking sheet and bake it for 20 minutes, turning it once halfway through. Lower the temperature to 350°F (175°C) and bake it for 30 to 40 minutes more, until the crust is golden and fully baked and the juices have thickened (you'll see them bubbling up through the steam vents in the top crust). Remove the pie to a rack to cool completely, at least 1 hour. This pie can be refrigerated for up to 1 week, covered in plastic wrap. Let it come to room temperature before serving, or warm it in a low oven. It can be kept frozen for up to 2 months: Wrap it in plastic, then in foil, and let it come to room temperature before serving.

A PIE STACK: Toasted Coconut Cream
Pie atop Pineapple Pie (page 69)

Classic Pie Crust (page 38)
    for one 9-inch (23-cm) pie

FILLING

1/3 cup (65 g) granulated sugar

1/4 cup (30 g) unbleached
    all-purpose flour

1/4 teaspoon salt

1 large egg

1 (14-ounce/414-ml) can
    coconut milk (not light;
    organic preferred)

1 cup half-and-half

1 cup (71 g) toasted shredded
    coconut (see Note: if
    using unsweetened,
    increase sugar to
    1/2 cup/100 g)

1 teaspoon vanilla extract

TOPPING

1 cup (240 ml) heavy cream

2 tablespoons powdered sugar

1 teaspoon vanilla extract

1/4 cup (15 g) toasted
    shredded coconut (see
    Note)

TOASTED COCONUT CREAM PIE

Preheat the oven to 425°F (220°C). Roll out the dough into a circle about 11 inches (28 cm) in diameter. Transfer it to a 9-inch (23-cm) pie plate, trim the overhang to about 1 inch (2.5 cm), tuck the overhang under, and crimp decoratively. Blind-bake the pie crust until fully baked (see page 35); set it aside to cool.

Make the filling: In a large, heavy-bottomed saucepan, whisk together the granulated sugar, flour, and salt until blended. Whisk in the egg, coconut milk, and half-and-half until fully combined and lump-free. Cook the mixture over medium heat, whisking frequently, until the custard comes to a boil and is thick, about 5 minutes. Remove the pan from the heat, and stir in the coconut and vanilla.

Put the fully baked crust on a baking sheet. Pour the filling into the crust, cover it with plastic wrap (allow the plastic to touch the surface of the filling), and refrigerate until the filling is fully cooled, about 4 hours.

Make the topping: In a stand mixer, with a hand mixer, or by hand with a whisk, whip the cream with the powdered sugar and vanilla until stiff peaks form. Spread it over the pie, top with the coconut, and serve.

NOTE To toast coconut, pour it onto a baking sheet and bake it at 350°F (175°C), stirring every few minutes, until it is golden, 10 to 15 minutes.

The coconut obsessive in me could eat this every day for breakfast. Thankfully, I have a small measure of impulse control, and usually manage to save it for dessert. The use of coconut milk in the pudding filling really makes the true flavor of coconut shine through, and the saltiness of my classic dough crust is the perfect foil to its rich sweetness.

MAKES one 9-inch (23-cm) pie

MINT JULEP CREAM PIE

I'm not a Southern gal, and I'm not a big expert on horse races, but I do know how to mix a mean cocktail, and mint juleps are a favorite of mine. I look forward to Kentucky Derby season every year for that reason (and for the ladies' amazingly ornate hats!). Always looking to transform my favorite flavors into pie recipes, I decided to take on this cocktail, and the result is light, minty, and oh-so-boozy. This is not a pie for kids.

MAKES   one 9-inch (23-cm) pie

Classic Pie Crust (page 38) for one 9-inch (23-cm) pie

Egg wash (page 25) or milk, for glaze

FILLING

3 large eggs

1/2 cup (110 g) firmly packed light brown sugar

1 cup (240 ml) mint simple syrup (recipe follows)

1/4 cup (60 ml) good-quality bourbon (I like Maker's Mark)

1/4 teaspoon salt

TOPPING

1 cup (240 ml) heavy cream

2 tablespoons mint simple syrup

Fresh or candied mint leaves (optional; recipe follows)

Preheat the oven to 425°F (220°C). Roll out the dough into a circle about 11 inches (28 cm) in diameter. Transfer it to a 9-inch (23-cm) pie plate, trim the overhang to about 1 inch (2.5 cm), tuck the overhang under, and crimp decoratively. Blind-bake the pie crust until partially baked (see page 35); set it aside to cool. Lower the oven to 350°F (175°C).

Brush the pie shell edges with egg wash or milk.

Make the filling: Whisk together the eggs and sugar until fully blended. Whisk in the syrup, bourbon, and salt.

Put the par-baked crust on a baking sheet. Pour the filling into the crust and bake for 20 to 25 minutes, until the filling has just set and is still slightly wobbly in the center. Remove the pie to cool completely.

Make the topping: In a stand mixer, with a hand mixer, or by hand with a whisk, whip the cream with the syrup until stiff peaks form. Pile the whipped cream on top of the cooled pie, and refrigerate until ready to serve, at least 30 minutes. Top the pie with fresh or candied mint leaves, if using, just before serving.

RECIPE CONTINUES

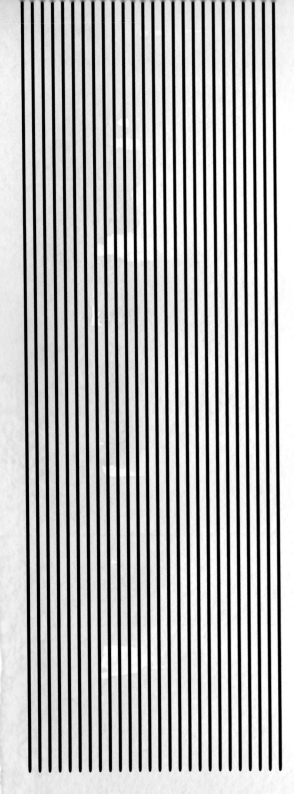

MINT SIMPLE SYRUP

I highly recommend doubling this recipe and saving some syrup for cocktails, or a killer mint lemonade!

1 cup (200 g) sugar

2 cups (50 g) fresh mint leaves (do not use the stems)

In a saucepan, heat the sugar with 1 cup (240 ml) water until just boiling (stir occasionally to fully dissolve the sugar). Remove from the heat and immediately stir in the mint. Allow the mint to steep for at least 30 minutes. Strain and refrigerate the syrup. It can be kept refrigerated for up to 1 week. To store longer, add 1 teaspoon vodka.

CANDIED MINT LEAVES

1/4 cup (50 g) sugar

1 egg white

A few pretty mint leaves

Pour the sugar onto a plate or shallow bowl. Whisk the egg white until frothy. Using a pastry brush, lightly coat the mint leaves with egg white, then dredge them in the sugar, tap off any excess, and let the leaves harden on a wire rack at room temperature for at least 3 hours. The candied leaves may be stored in an airtight container for up to 2 days.

Classic Pie Crust (page 38) for one 9-inch (23-cm) pie

FILLING

2 (12-ounce/355-ml) bottles Guinness Extra Stout beer

3 large eggs

1/2 cup (110 g) firmly packed light brown sugar

1 cup (240 ml) Bailey's Irish Cream

1/4 cup (60 ml) barley malt syrup

1/4 teaspoon salt

Egg wash (page 25) or milk, for glaze

TOPPING

1 cup (240 ml) heavy cream

2 tablespoons Jameson Irish Whiskey

2 tablespoons Bailey's Irish Cream

IRISH CAR BOMB CREAM PIE

Preheat the oven to 425°F (220°C). Roll out the dough into a circle about 11 inches (28 cm) in diameter. Transfer it to a 9-inch (23-cm) pie plate, trim the overhang to about 1 inch (2.5 cm), tuck the overhang under, and crimp decoratively. Blind-bake the pie crust until partially baked (see page 35); set it aside to cool. Lower the oven to 350°F (175°C).

Brush the pie shell edges with egg wash or milk.

Make the filling: Bring the beer to a boil and cook on high until it is reduced to about 1/2 cup (120 ml), 15 to 20 minutes. Allow it to cool before using. Set aside 1 tablespoon for the topping.

In a bowl, whisk together the eggs and sugar until fully blended. Whisk in the Bailey's, the malt syrup, the remaining 1/2 cup (120 ml) Guinness syrup, and the salt.

Put the par-baked crust on a baking sheet. Pour the filling into the crust and bake for 20 to 25 minutes, until the filling has just set and is still slightly wobbly in the center. Remove the pie to cool completely.

Make the topping: In a stand mixer, with a hand mixer, or by hand with a whisk, whip the cream with the Jameson and Bailey's until stiff peaks form. Pile it on top of the cooled pie, drizzle with the reserved Guinness syrup, and serve immediately. Otherwise, refrigerate it until ready to serve, and drizzle the syrup over the top right before serving. This pie can be refrigerated for up to 1 week without the topping, covered in plastic wrap. Make the topping right before serving.

Ah, the Irish Car Bomb. A popular tipple on St. Patrick's Day, or whenever you want to speed up the inebriation process, this drink consists of a shot of Jameson Irish Whiskey and Bailey's Irish Cream, dropped into a pint of Guinness, and consumed in one go. It's insane. It's also delicious. So is this pie.

MAKES one 9-inch (23-cm) pie

Chocolate Cookie Crust
(page 58) for one 9-inch
(23-cm) pie

FILLING
2 cups (270 g) Nutella

1¹/₂ cups (338 g) mascarpone
cheese

¹/₄ teaspoon salt

TOPPING
¹/₂ cup (55 g) chopped toasted
hazelnuts

Preheat the oven to 350°F (175°C). Pat the crust into a 9-inch (23-cm) pie plate. Bake it for 10 minutes, then let it cool completely.

Make the filling: In a large bowl, using a hand mixer, or in the bowl of a stand mixer fitted with the whisk attachment, beat together the Nutella, mascarpone, and salt until light and fluffy. Spread the filling into the pie shell, cover it with plastic wrap, and refrigerate until firm, about 1 hour.

Top the pie with the chopped nuts, slice the pie, and serve. This pie can be refrigerated for up to 1 week, covered in plastic wrap (but it won't last that long!).

NUTELLA PIE*

If you've never tried Nutella, that ambrosial combination of hazelnuts and chocolate, put this book down right now, run to your nearest grocery store, and buy a jar. Bring a spoon along to expedite the Nutella-in-mouth process. OK, now that we're all on the same Nutella-obsession page, I'll proceed with a recipe that will make you fall into an incoherent puddle of babbling ecstasy, while simultaneously making you the most popular of all your friends (if you can bring yourself to share). What's more, this is a speedy, incredibly easy one to whip up, so you don't have to delay your satisfaction for too long.

MAKES one 9-inch (23-cm) pie

June

June marks the beginning of summer and
the first hint of the goodness to come. Look
out for ripe strawberries, and the first
peek of blueberries coming into season,
and an explosion of fresh herbs.

IIIIIIIIIIIIIIIIIIIIIIIIIIIIIIIIIII

STRAWBERRY-BASIL PIE

Sounds weird? Trust me, you won't be thinking that when you take a bite. Inspired by a riff on the classic Italian caprese salad, in which strawberries fill in for tomatoes, this pie is fragrant, tart, and absolutely delicious. Ingredients you might normally find in a salad bowl (balsamic vinegar, sage, black pepper) find a happy home in this pie, which is one of my most popular summer specialties!

MAKES one 9-inch (23-cm) pie

Classic Pie (page 38) or Cornmeal Crust (page 44) for one double-crust 9-inch (23-cm) pie

FILLING

8 cups (1.2 kg) fresh strawberries, hulled and halved (cut large berries into smaller pieces)

About 10 large fresh basil leaves, julienned

3 tablespoons high-quality balsamic vinegar

Zest of 1 lemon

3/4 cup (150 g) sugar

1/4 cup (30 g) cornstarch

1 teaspoon freshly ground black pepper

1/4 teaspoon salt

Egg wash (page 25) or milk, for glaze

Raw sugar, for garnish

Preheat the oven to 425°F (220°C). Roll out half of the dough into a circle about 11 inches (28 cm) in diameter. Transfer it to a 9-inch (23-cm) pie plate. Trim the overhang to 1 inch (2.5 cm) and refrigerate the crust.

Make the filling: In a large bowl, toss together the strawberries, basil, vinegar, and lemon zest. In a separate bowl, mix together the sugar, cornstarch, pepper, and salt. Just before adding the filling to the crust, toss the fruit in the dry ingredients. Brush the rim of the bottom crust with egg wash or milk.

Roll out the second half of the dough into a circle about 11 inches (28 cm) in diameter. Cut it into six 2-inch- (5-cm-) thick strips. Form a lattice (see page 30). Trim the edges, and tuck the top crust over the rim of the bottom crust to form a tight seal. Crimp the edge into whatever pattern you like. Brush the top crust with egg wash or milk, and sprinkle it with raw sugar.

Put the pie on a baking sheet and bake it for 20 minutes, turning it once halfway through. Lower the temperature to 350°F (175°C) and bake it for 30 to 40 minutes more, until the crust is golden and fully baked and the juices have thickened. Remove the pie to a rack to cool completely, at least 1 hour. This pie can be refrigerated for up to 1 week, covered in plastic wrap. Let it come to room temperature before serving, or warm it in a low oven. It can be kept frozen for up to 2 months: Cover it in plastic wrap, then in foil, and let it come to room temperature before serving.

ROCKY ROAD PIE

One of my favorite ice cream flavors—now one of my favorite pies! Feel free to toss in coconut or different nuts, or use all milk instead of dark chocolate. This is an endlessly adaptable recipe, and the idea is to have a delightful, gooey mess on your plate!

MAKES one 9-inch (23-cm) pie

Chocolate Cookie Crust
   (page 58) for one 9-inch
   (23-cm) pie

FILLING

4 ounces (115 g) bittersweet
   chocolate, chopped

4 ounces (115 g) milk
   chocolate, chopped

1 cup (240 ml) heavy cream

1 large egg, at room
   temperature

1/2 teaspoon salt

1/2 cup (55 g) chopped cashews
   (walnuts, almonds,
   pecans, or peanuts work
   too!)

1 cup (85 g) marshmallow fluff
   (see page 131), warmed
   (see Note)

Preheat the oven to 350°F (175°C). Pat the crust into a 9-inch (23-cm) pie plate. Bake it for 10 minutes, then let it cool completely.

Make the filling: Put both chocolates in a heatproof bowl. In a saucepan, heat the cream over medium-high heat until it is scalded but not boiling. Pour the cream over the chocolate and let it stand for 1 minute. Whisk together the hot cream and the chocolate until they are fully blended into a glossy ganache. Whisk in the egg and salt. Stir in half of the nuts and half of the marshmallow fluff (but don't overstir; you want to see the swirls of marshmallow).

Put the crust on a baking sheet. Pour the filling into the crust and bake for 20 to 25 minutes, until the filling has just set and is still slightly wobbly in the center. Remove the pie to cool completely.

When the pie has cooled, pour the remaining marshmallow fluff over the pie, sprinkle on the remaining nuts, and allow the topping to cool until set. This pie can be refrigerated for up to 1 week, covered in plastic wrap.

NOTE To warm the marshmallow fluff, put it in a microwave-safe bowl and heat it for 30 seconds on high, then stir and repeat until it's loose. You can also heat it in a saucepan on the stove over medium heat, stirring frequently, until it's pourable.

Classic Pie (page 38) or
    Cornmeal Crust (page 44)
    for one double-crust
    9-inch (23-cm) pie

FILLING

1 pound (455 g) fresh
    nectarines (about 4),
    cored and sliced

4 cups (560 g) fresh
    blueberries

Zest of 1 lemon

1 teaspoon vanilla extract

$^3/_4$ cup (150 g) sugar

$^1/_4$ cup (30 g) cornstarch

$^1/_4$ teaspoon cinnamon

$^1/_4$ teaspoon salt

Egg wash (page 25) or milk,
    for glaze

Raw sugar, for garnish

Preheat the oven to 425°F (220°C). Roll out half of the dough into a circle about 11 inches (28 cm) in diameter. Transfer it to a 9-inch (23-cm) pie plate. Trim the overhang to 1 inch (2.5 cm) and refrigerate the crust.

Make the filling: In a large bowl, toss together the nectarines, berries, lemon zest, and vanilla. In a separate bowl, mix together the sugar, cornstarch, cinnamon, and salt. Just before adding the filling to the pie plate, toss the fruit in the dry ingredients. Brush the rim of the bottom crust with egg wash or milk.

Roll out the second half of the dough into a circle about 11 inches (28 cm) in diameter. Lay it over the filled pie. Trim the edges, and tuck the top crust over the rim of the bottom crust to form a tight seal. Crimp the edge into whatever pattern you like. Brush the top crust with egg wash or milk, sprinkle it with raw sugar, and cut a few slits to allow steam to escape.

Put the pie on a baking sheet and bake it for 20 minutes, turning it once halfway through. Lower the temperature to 350°F (175°C) and bake it for 30 to 40 minutes more, until the crust is golden and fully baked and the juices have thickened. Remove the pie to a rack to cool completely, at least 1 hour. This pie can be refrigerated for up to 1 week, covered in plastic wrap. Let it come to room temperature before serving, or warm it in a low oven. It can be kept frozen for up to 2 months: Wrap it in plastic, then in foil, and let it come to room temperature before serving.

BLUEBERRY-NECTARINE PIE

There's nothing like a simple slice of blueberry pie, but I'd argue that tossing in some nectarines ups the flavor ante even more. If you want to go with tradition, just omit the nectarines and double the blueberries— you'll be smiling either way.

MAKES one 9-inch (23-cm) pie

Classic Pie Crust (page 38) for one 9-inch (23-cm) pie

FILLING

$1^{1}/_{2}$ cups (135 g) roasted, unsalted macadamia nuts (coarsely chop 1 cup; leave the rest whole)

1 (14-ounce/414-ml) can coconut milk, chilled

$1^{1}/_{2}$ cups (300 g) sugar

$^{1}/_{2}$ cup (120 ml) super-strong brewed Kona coffee (or espresso, dark roast, etc.)

$^{1}/_{4}$ cup (60 ml) light corn syrup

$^{1}/_{2}$ cup (1 stick/115 g) unsalted butter

1 cup (75 g) coconut flakes, toasted (see Note, page 93)

$^{1}/_{2}$ teaspoon salt

HAWAIIAN DELIGHT PIE

Preheat the oven to 425°F (220°C). Roll out the dough into a circle about 11 inches (28 cm) in diameter. Transfer it to a 9-inch (23-cm) pie plate, trim the overhang to about 1 inch (2.5 cm), tuck the overhang under, and crimp decoratively. Blind-bake the pie crust until fully baked (see page 35); set it aside to cool.

Make the filling: In a skillet, toast the macadamia nuts over low heat, tossing regularly, until they are fragrant and lightly toasted (watch them so they don't burn). Set them aside.

Open the coconut milk, spoon the firm coconut cream from the top, and keep it handy. Discard the remaining coconut water.

In a saucepan over medium-high heat, stir together the sugar, coffee, and corn syrup until the sugar has dissolved. Cook the caramel until a candy thermometer reads 350°F (175°C), or until it is a deep brown.

Remove the caramel from the heat and immediately whisk in the reserved coconut cream. Be careful to avoid the hot steam that will release when the cream hits the caramel. Continue to whisk and add in the butter. Once the butter is melted, stir in the macadamia nuts, coconut, and salt. Pour the filling into the pie shell and allow it to cool completely, at least 4 hours. Enjoy a slice with a cup of Kona coffee! This pie can be refrigerated for up to 1 week, covered in plastic wrap. Let it come to room temperature before serving. For easier slicing, run your knife first under hot water to prevent the caramel from sticking to the blade.

While writing this book, I had the incredible fortune to spend two weeks in Hawaii, on the island of Oahu. During that time, I found myself in the town of Kailua, in my friends' incredible home, taking care of Goose (their springer spaniel) and testing recipes in their massive kitchen. This recipe was born of that time, and incorporates many of the flavors that make Hawaiian cuisine so special. You don't have to use Kona coffee in this recipe; any strong-flavored dark roast will do, but I love to support the local agriculture of Hawaii by using their regional beans. Enjoy!

MAKES one 9-inch (23-cm) pie

STRAWBERRY SHORTCAKE PIE

Strawberry shortcake is one of my favorite desserts of all time. It's all about the freshness of in-season strawberries, in all their tart, fragrant glory. Make this one when strawberries are at their ripest, and try to get those insanely good little "Tristar" berries from your local farmers' market if you can! The buttermilk biscuit pie crust for this recipe is really something special.

MAKES one 9-inch (23-cm) pie

FILLING
8 cups (1.2 kg) fresh strawberries, hulled and halved (cut large berries into quarters)

$^1/_2$ cup (100 g) sugar

Zest of 1 lemon

$^1/_4$ teaspoon salt

$1^1/_2$ cups (360 ml) heavy cream

1 teaspoon vanilla extract

BISCUIT PIE CRUST
8 ounces (225 g/approximately 2 cups) unbleached all-purpose flour

1 tablespoon baking powder

$^1/_2$ teaspoon salt

$^1/_4$ teaspoon baking soda

Zest of 1 orange

6 tablespoons ($^3/_4$ stick/85 g) unsalted butter, cubed and frozen

1 cup (240 ml) buttermilk

Egg wash (page 25) or milk, for glaze

Make the filling: In a large bowl, toss together the strawberries, ¼ cup (100 g) of the sugar, the lemon zest, and salt. Set them aside to macerate and develop juices while you prepare the dough.

Make the crust: In a large bowl or the work bowl of a food processor, toss or pulse the flour, baking powder, salt, and baking soda together. Cut or pulse in the zest and butter until the mixture resembles coarse meal. Drizzle in the buttermilk and toss or pulse until the dough is just combined. It should be quite wet; add a bit more buttermilk if necessary.

On a floured surface, pat the dough together and fold it over itself, patting and pressing four or five times, until it comes together. Using a floured rolling pin, roll the dough out to 1 inch (2.5 cm) thick and transfer it to a 9-inch (23-cm) pie plate. Trim the overhang to 1 inch (2.5 cm). (You can reshape the excess dough to cut into biscuits or free-form strips. You can bake these separately and eat them on their own or layer them in your pie. They can also be frozen for later use.)

Fold the dough overhang under the outer edge and crimp. Prick the bottom of the dough all over with a fork, and freeze it for about 15 minutes.

Preheat the oven to 425°F (220°C).

Line the pie dough with foil or parchment, fill it with dried beans or pie weights, and bake it for 20 minutes, rotating it once halfway through (see page 35 for blind-baking tips). Lower the temperature to 350°F (175°C), remove the foil and weights, brush the crust with egg wash or milk; and bake it for another 10 to 20 minutes, until the biscuit is golden and fluffy. Remove it to cool completely.

In a stand mixer, with a hand mixer, or by hand with a whisk, whip together the heavy cream, vanilla, and remaining ¼ cup (100 g) sugar until stiff peaks form. Spread a layer of whipped cream in the bottom of the crust, then a layer of berries, and repeat, alternating, until you have a big, fluffy, messy, beautiful pile of berries and cream in your biscuit crust. Slice and serve it immediately. The crust can be refrigerated for up to 2 days, covered in plastic wrap. Wait to assemble the pie until just before serving.

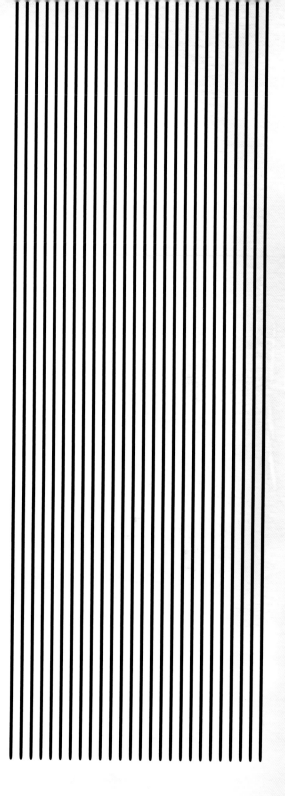

MELOPITA (GREEK HONEY & CHEESE PIE)

I first heard of this Greek specialty when looking for a twist on a classic farmer's cheese pie. The ingredients in this pie are very simple, so quality is of utmost importance. Use a very flavorful honey, such as wildflower, and if you can't find myzithra cheese at your local Greek or cheese specialty shop, whole-milk ricotta makes an excellent substitute. Homemade ricotta (believe me, it's easy!) is an especially nice touch in this pie.

MAKES   one 9-inch (23-cm) pie

Classic Pie Crust (page 38) for one 9-inch (23-cm) pie

FILLING

³/₄ pound (341 g) soft myzithra or ricotta cheese (recipe follows)

3 large eggs, lightly beaten

³/₄ cup (180 ml) wildflower honey (or any extremely flavorful honey)

3 tablespoons all-purpose flour

Zest of 1 lemon

¹/₂ teaspoon cinnamon (plus extra for decoration, if desired)

¹/₄ teaspoon salt

Egg wash (page 25) or milk, for glaze

Preheat the oven to 425°F (220°C). Roll out the dough into a circle about 11 inches (28 cm) in diameter. Transfer it to a 9-inch (23-cm) pie plate, trim the overhang to about 1 inch (2.5 cm), tuck the overhang under, and crimp decoratively. Blind-bake the pie crust until partially baked (see page 35); set it aside to cool. Lower the oven to 350°F (175°C).

Make the filling: In a large bowl, whisk together the cheese and eggs until fully blended. Whisk in the honey, flour, lemon zest, cinnamon, and salt until fully incorporated.

Put the pie crust on a baking sheet. Brush the crust edges with egg wash or milk. Pour in the filling, and bake the pie for 30 to 40 minutes, until the filling has just set and is still slightly wobbly in the center. Remove the pie to cool completely on a wire rack, at least 1 hour. If desired, dust the surface of the pie with cinnamon. This pie can be refrigerated for up to 1 week, covered in plastic wrap.

HOMEMADE RICOTTA RECIPE

MAKES approximately 18 ounces (2 cups) of cheese

1 quart (960 ml) whole
    milk (avoid the ultra-
    pasteurized kind)

1 pint (480 ml) heavy cream

1 teaspoon sea salt

3 tablespoons freshly
    squeezed lemon juice or
    white wine vinegar

Over a large, deep bowl, set a sieve lined with fine-weave cheesecloth. In a steel or enamel pot, mix together the milk, cream, and salt. Bring the mixture to a full boil over medium heat, stirring occasionally to prevent the milk from burning. Turn off the heat, stir in the lemon juice, and allow the mixture to stand for a couple of minutes until it has curdled (divided into curds and whey).

Pour the mixture into the cheesecloth and allow it to drain into the bowl for 20 to 30 minutes, depending on the desired texture (the longer it drains the drier and more dense it becomes). Use it right away, or wrap the cheese in plastic and refrigerate it for up to 5 days.

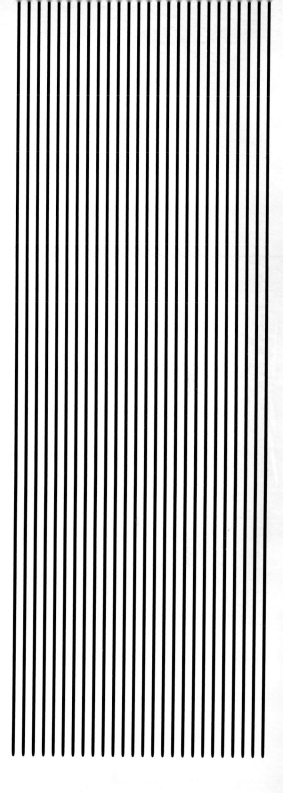

July

Things are really heating up now. You're
hitting the beach, working on your tan (or in
my case, freckles), reveling in the piles of
berries at your farmers' market, and eating
ice cream at every possible opportunity...

BANANA SPLIT ICE CREAM 114

LICORICIOUS 117

BERRY MEDLEY 118

RASPBERRY VINEGAR TART 120

GRASSHOPPER 122

SOUR CHERRY 124

GREEN TOMATO 125

CONE CRUST

10 to 15 sugar ice cream cones

5 to 8 tablespoons (70 to 115 g) unsalted butter, melted

FILLING

1 cup (240 ml) chocolate ice cream, slightly softened (see Note)

4 medium-ripe bananas, sliced lengthwise

1 cup (240 ml) vanilla ice cream, slightly softened (see Note)

$^1/_2$ cup (55 g) chopped toasted walnuts

TOPPING

1 cup (240 ml) heavy cream

2 tablespoons powdered sugar

1 teaspoon vanilla extract

$^1/_2$ cup (120 ml) warm hot fudge sauce (store-bought or see recipe that follows)

$^1/_4$ cup (30 g) chopped toasted walnuts

Maraschino cherries (optional)

Make the crust: Grind the ice cream cones in a food processor (or put them in a plastic bag and bash 'em with a rolling pin), until finely crumbled. Drizzle in the butter and mix until the texture is that of wet sand. Press the crust into a 9-inch (23-cm) pie plate and freeze it for about 5 minutes.

Make the filling: Spread half of the chocolate ice cream over the bottom of the cone crust. Lay half of the banana slices over the ice cream, and top with half of the vanilla ice cream. Sprinkle in the walnuts, and repeat the layers as above.

Make the topping: In a stand mixer, with a hand mixer, or by hand with a whisk, whip the cream, sugar, and vanilla until stiff peaks form. Spread the whipped cream over the pie and drizzle it with the hot fudge and nuts. Don't forget the cherry on top! This pie can be frozen, without the topping, for up to 2 weeks, covered tightly in plastic wrap. Allow it to warm up for 5 to 10 minutes before topping, slicing, and serving.

NOTE To soften the ice cream for this recipe, allow it to sit at room temperature for about 15 minutes, until the ice cream is soft enough to scoop and spread, but not soupy.

RECIPE CONTINUES

BANANA SPLIT ICE CREAM PIE

Full disclosure time: I might be a pie baker, but ice cream is my kryptonite. Fortunately, this recipe lets me have my pie and eat my ice cream too. Approach this as you would a sundae bar: Use whatever ice cream flavors, sauces, nuts, candies, and toppings float your boat. I'm basing this on the classic banana split, but I encourage you to play around and experiment with this fun, delicious, and dead-simple recipe!

MAKES one 9-inch (23-cm) pie

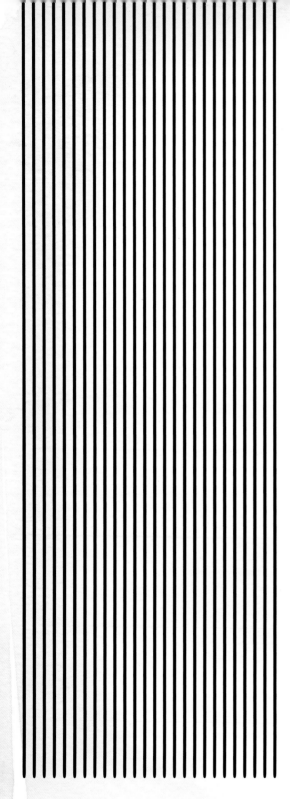

HOMEMADE HOT FUDGE SAUCE

MAKES approximately 1 ½ cups (355 ml) of sauce

$^1/_2$ cup (120 ml) heavy cream

4 ounces (115 g) bittersweet chocolate, chopped or chips

$^1/_2$ cup (100 g) sugar

1 tablespoon butter

$^1/_4$ teaspoon salt

1 teaspoon vanilla extract

In a heavy-bottomed saucepan, heat the cream over medium heat until it is hot but not boiling. Stir in the chocolate, sugar, butter, and salt until they are fully dissolved. Continue to cook the sauce over medium heat until it is smooth and heated through. Remove it from the heat and stir in the vanilla. Use it immediately or refrigerate it for up to 2 weeks.

Classic Pie Crust (page 38)
    for one 9-inch (23-cm) pie

FILLING

5 cups (1.2 L) whole milk

½ cup (113 g) finely chopped
    black licorice (see Note)

6 tablespoons (45 g)
    cornstarch

4 large eggs

½ cup (1 stick/115 g)
    unsalted butter

2 cups (440 g) firmly packed
    light brown sugar

1 teaspoon sea salt

1 tablespoon absinthe or
    Pernod

TOPPING

1 cup (240 ml) heavy cream

2 tablespoons powdered sugar

1 tablespoon absinthe or
    Pernod

LICORICIOUS PIE

Licorice. It's a love-it-or-hate-it thing. If you're on Team Hate It, go ahead and turn the page. If you, like me, are on Team LOVE IT, have I got a recipe for you. Creamy, licorice-infused pudding, with a good hit of salt and a splash of absinthe—licorice lovers will think they've died and gone to heaven.

MAKES one 9-inch (23-cm) pie

Preheat the oven to 425°F (220°C). Roll out the dough into a circle about 11 inches (28 cm) in diameter. Transfer it to a 9-inch (23-cm) pie plate, trim the overhang to about 1 inch (2.5 cm), tuck the overhang under, and crimp decoratively. Blind-bake the pie crust until fully baked (see page 35); set it aside to cool.

Make the filling: In a large saucepan, heat the milk with the licorice, over medium-high heat, stirring occasionally, until the milk is scalded. Remove it from the heat and set it aside to steep, for at least 30 minutes. If the licorice hasn't fully dissolved in that time, strain it out or keep it in for a little surprise while you're eating!

Once the milk has steeped and cooled, ladle out about ½ cup (120 ml) of it into a small bowl, and whisk it together with the cornstarch. Once it is fully combined, whisk in the eggs. Set the mixture aside.

In a large saucepan, melt the butter over medium-high heat. Mix in the brown sugar and salt, and stir until combined and lightly caramelized. Remove it from the heat.

Whisk the remaining portion of milk into the butter-and-sugar mixture (the sugar may seize up a bit; don't worry, it will melt again). Whisk in the cornstarch-egg mixture. Return the pan to medium-high heat and bring it to a boil, whisking frequently. Once it begins to boil, lower the heat to a simmer and whisk constantly until the pudding has thickened, about 7 minutes.

Remove the pan from the heat, whisk in the absinthe, and pour the filling into the pie shell. Refrigerate it, with plastic wrap pressed to the surface of the pudding, until it is fully chilled and set (3 to 4 hours).

Make the topping: In a stand mixer, with a hand mixer, or by hand with a whisk, whip the cream with the powdered sugar and absinthe until stiff peaks form. Spread the whipped cream over the filling, slice the pie, and serve.

NOTE When selecting your licorice, use the good stuff. The hard, pellet-like candies from Italy or the Netherlands are perfect. You can also use the softer kinds like Panda or Kookaburra. Skip the Twizzlers this time. If using salted licorice, lower the salt content of the filling to ¼ teaspoon.

BERRY MEDLEY PIE

At the height of summer, when fresh berries are at their finest, I like to mix them all up together in this delicious pie. Don't mess with Mother Nature—a minimal amount of intervention lets the fruit really shine.

MAKES   one 9-inch (23-cm) pie

Classic Pie (page 38) or Cornmeal Crust (page 44) for one double-crust 9-inch (23-cm) pie

FILLING

4 cups (608 g) fresh strawberries, hulled and halved (cut large berries into smaller pieces)

4 cups (560 g) fresh blueberries

2 cups (304 g) fresh raspberries

2 cups (288 g) fresh blackberries

Zest of 1 lemon

1 teaspoon vanilla extract

3/4 cup (150 g) sugar

1/4 cup (30 g) cornstarch

1/4 teaspoon salt

Egg wash (page 25) or milk, for glaze

Raw sugar, for garnish

Preheat the oven to 425°F (220°C). Roll out half of the dough into a circle about 11 inches (28 cm) in diameter. Transfer it to a 9-inch (23-cm) pie plate. Trim the overhang to 1 inch (2.5 cm) and refrigerate the crust.

Make the filling: In a large bowl, toss together the berries, lemon zest, and vanilla. In a separate bowl, mix together the sugar, cornstarch, and salt. Just before adding the filling to the pie plate, toss the fruit in the dry ingredients. Brush the rim of the bottom crust with egg wash or milk.

Roll out the second half of the dough into a circle about 11 inches (28 cm) in diameter. Cut it into lattice strips, and arrange them over the filled pie (see page 30). Trim the edges and tuck the top crust over the rim of the bottom crust to form a tight seal. Crimp the edge into whatever pattern you like. Brush the top crust with egg wash or milk, and sprinkle it with the raw sugar.

Put the pie on a baking sheet and bake it for 20 minutes, turning it once halfway through. Lower the temperature to 350°F (175°C) and bake it for 30 to 40 minutes more, until the crust is golden and fully baked and the juices have thickened (you'll see them bubbling out through the lattice crust). Remove the pie to a rack to cool completely, at least 1 hour. This pie can be refrigerated for up to 1 week, covered in plastic wrap. Let it come to room temperature before serving, or warm it in a low oven. It can be kept frozen for up to 2 months: Wrap it in plastic, then in foil, and let it come to room temperature before serving.

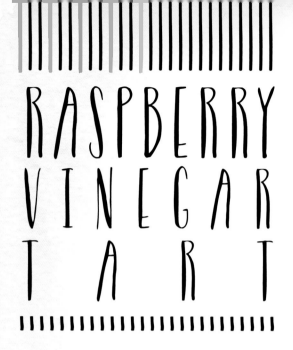

RASPBERRY VINEGAR TART

A version of this recipe appeared in the *New York Times Magazine* in 2010, for Amanda Hesser's *"Recipe Redux"* column. Amanda had an old recipe for a raspberry shrub beverage (shrubs are tart, vinegar-based drinks that were very popular at the turn of the twentieth century), which I used as inspiration for this pie. Vinegar pies were very popular in the States back when citrus fruits were expensive and hard to come by. A couple of tablespoons of vinegar make a fine substitute for lemon juice in a chess pie (see page 90), providing a nice sour kick. I took that concept and ran with it, but of course I had to fancy it up with chocolate, raspberries, and elderflower liqueur!

MAKES   one 9-inch (23-cm) pie

Chocolate Cookie (page 58) or Chocolate Pie Crust (page 47) for one 9-inch (23-cm) pie

FILLING

2 large eggs

1 cup (200 g) sugar

1 tablespoon unbleached all-purpose flour

2 tablespoons red wine vinegar

1 tablespoon raspberry vinegar (store-bought or see recipe that follows)

TOPPING

1 cup (240 ml) heavy cream

2 tablespoons raspberry vinegar, plus extra for garnish

1 tablespoon elderflower liqueur (St. Germain is excellent)

For the **Chocolate Cookie Crust**, preheat the oven to 350°F (175°C), pat the crust into a 9-inch (23-cm) pie pan, refrigerate for 5 minutes, then bake it for 10 minutes and allow it to cool completely. For the **Chocolate Pie Crust**, preheat the oven to 425°F (220°C), and roll out the dough into a circle about 11 inches (28 cm) in diameter. Transfer it to a 9-inch (23-cm) tart pan or pie plate, trim the overhang to about 1 inch (2.5 cm), fold the overhang under, and crimp decoratively. Blind-bake the crust until partially baked (see page 35); set it aside to cool. Lower the oven to 350°F (175°C).

Make the filling: In a large bowl, whisk together the eggs and ¼ cup (50 g) of the sugar.

In a medium, heavy-bottomed saucepan, whisk together the flour and remaining ¾ cup (150 g) of the sugar, then whisk in 1 cup (240 ml) cold water and the vinegars. Bring them to a boil, whisking until the sugar is dissolved, then add the mixture to the egg bowl in a slow, steady stream, whisking constantly to prevent the eggs from scrambling. Pour the filling back into the saucepan and cook it over medium heat, stirring constantly, until it coats the back of a wooden spoon, 12 to 15 minutes. Do not let it boil.

Put the crust on a baking sheet. Pour the filling into the crust and bake until the filling has just set and is still slightly wobbly in the center, about 20 minutes. Remove the pie to cool completely, then refrigerate it.

Make the topping: In a stand mixer, with a hand mixer, or by hand with a whisk, whip the cream with the vinegar and liqueur until stiff peaks form. Spread the whipped cream over the filling, then drizzle it with more raspberry vinegar. This pie can be made ahead, without the topping, and refrigerated for up to 1 week, covered in plastic wrap. Make the topping just before serving.

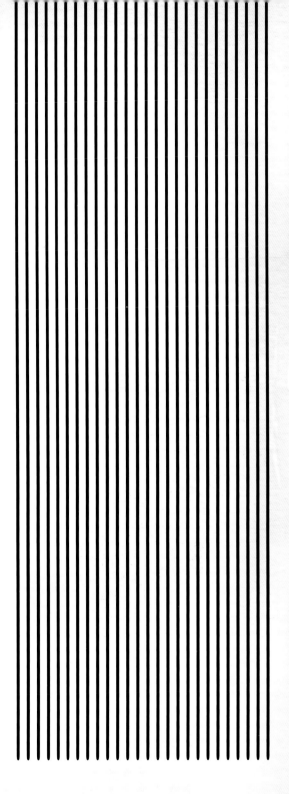

RASPBERRY VINEGAR

This will make more than you need for this recipe. Use the rest in cocktails, or just mix it with some seltzer for a tart, refreshing drink.

MAKES   about 1 cup (240 ml) vinegar syrup

¹/₄ cup (60 ml) red wine
    vinegar

2 cups fresh red raspberries

Sugar, as needed

In a nonreactive bowl, combine the vinegar and raspberries. Cover and let them macerate at room temperature for 3 days.

Mash the raspberries in the bowl and strain the liquid through a fine-mesh sieve lined with cheesecloth. To every 1 cup (240 ml) juice, add 8 ounces (225 g) sugar. Combine the juice and sugar in a saucepan. Bring them to a boil and simmer (gently!) for 15 minutes. Let the mixture cool, then bottle it. Keep it refrigerated for up to 3 months.

GRASSHOPPER PIE

Chocolate Cookie Crust
(page 58) for one 9-inch
(23-cm) pie

FILLING

1 1/2 cups (200 g) marshmallow
fluff (see page 131), or
24 large marshmallows

1/3 cup (75 ml) half-and-half

2 tablespoons clear crème de
menthe liqueur

2 tablespoons clear crème de
cacao liqueur

A few drops of green food
coloring (optional)

1 cup (240 ml) heavy cream

TOPPING

Crumbled chocolate cookies
or shaved dark chocolate
(optional)

Pat the crust into a 9-inch (23-cm) pie plate and freeze until ready to use.

Make the filling: Prepare an ice bath. In a heavy saucepan, heat the marshmallow fluff and half-and-half over medium heat, stirring constantly. As soon as the mixture has fully melted and combined, remove it from the heat and place it in the ice bath, stirring occasionally, until it is fully cooled (if you've got lots of time, you can skip this step and let it cool down in the fridge).

Stir in the liqueurs and the food coloring, if using, until the filling is a light mint shade of green.

In a stand mixer, with a hand mixer, or by hand with a whisk, whip the cream until stiff peaks form, and then gently fold the mint mixture into the cream until it is fully incorporated.

Pour the filling into the crust and freeze it, uncovered, until it's fully set, at least 2 hours. Once the pie has set, you can wrap it in plastic and then in foil to keep it frozen (it will last for up to 2 months in the freezer). To serve, let the pie sit at room temperature for about 10 minutes before slicing. Garnish slices with cookie crumbs or chocolate, if desired, just before serving.

NOTE This is an icebox pie, and is best when still slightly frozen and very cold. It will melt a bit if left at room temperature for too long.

I'm going to preface this recipe with a warning: There is no worse hangover on earth than a crème de menthe hangover. Do not make the mistake, as I did the first time I ever got truly drunk, of being seduced by the sweet minty-freshness of this liqueur. Too much is way too much. Now that you've been warned, I can tell you that a Grasshopper Pie makes beautiful use of this elixir. Every slice is a light, airy cloud of minty-chocolatey goodness. My recipe incorporates the gorgeous marshmallow fluff that I use for my beloved S'mores Pie. Make a double batch, make both pies, and be the most popular person at the party.

MAKES one 9-inch (23-cm) pie

SOUR CHERRY PIE

Sour cherries should just be called pie cherries; they were so clearly destined for this dessert. As their name suggests, these are much more tart than the dark red Bing cherries we all like to snack on, and aren't really suited to being eaten raw. Mix them up with some sugar and vanilla in a pie crust, however, and they sing. I like to dust a mix of flour, sugar, and ground almonds in the bottom of the pie before adding my cherries. It's delicious, and keeps the juices from making the bottom crust soggy.

Pro tip: Invest in a good cherry pitter if you plan to make more than one of these (and you'll want to make more than one).

MAKES   one 9-inch (23-cm) pie

Classic Pie (page 38), Cornmeal (page 44), or Chocolate Pie Crust (page 47) for one double-crust 9-inch (23-cm) pie

FILLING
$^1/_4$ cup (30 g) unbleached all-purpose flour

$^1/_4$ cup (50 g) granulated sugar

$^1/_4$ cup (30 g) slivered almonds, chopped or ground in the food processor

2 pounds (910 g) sour cherries, pitted

1 teaspoon vanilla extract

1 cup (220 g) firmly packed dark brown sugar

$^1/_4$ cup (30 g) cornstarch

$^1/_4$ teaspoon salt

Egg wash (page 25) or milk, for glaze

Raw sugar, for garnish

Preheat the oven to 425°F (220°C). Roll out half of the dough into a circle about 11 inches (28 cm) in diameter. Transfer it to a 9-inch (23-cm) pie plate. Trim the overhang to 1 inch (2.5 cm) and refrigerate the crust.

Make the filling: In a small bowl, mix together the flour, granulated sugar, and almonds.

In a large bowl, toss together the cherries and vanilla. In a separate bowl, mix together the brown sugar, cornstarch, and salt. Just before adding the filling to the pie plate, toss the fruit in the brown sugar mixture. Brush the rim of the bottom crust with egg wash or milk.

Put the bottom crust on a baking sheet. Pour the almond mixture into the crust. Pour the filling on top. Roll out the second half of the dough, cut it into lattice strips, and arrange them over the filled pie (see page 30). Trim the edges and tuck the top crust over the rim of the bottom crust to form a tight seal. Crimp the edge into whatever pattern you like. Brush the top crust with egg wash or milk and sprinkle it with raw sugar.

Bake the pie for 20 minutes, turning it once halfway through. Lower the temperature to 350°F (175°C) and bake it for 30 to 40 minutes more, until the crust is golden and fully baked and the juices have thickened. Remove the pie to a rack to cool completely, at least 1 hour. This pie can be refrigerated for up to 1 week, covered in plastic wrap. Let it come to room temperature before serving, or warm it in a low oven. It can be kept frozen for up to 2 months: Wrap it in plastic, then in foil, and let it come to room temperature before serving.

Classic Pie (page 38) or
    Cornmeal Crust (page 44)
    for one double-crust
    9-inch (23-cm) pie

FILLING

1 cup (220 g) firmly packed
    dark brown sugar

1/3 cup (40 g) cornstarch

1/2 teaspoon ground ginger

1/2 teaspoon cinnamon

1/4 teaspoon salt

2 pounds (910 g) green
    tomatoes

Egg wash (page 25) or milk,
    for glaze

Raw sugar, for garnish

Preheat the oven to 425°F (220°C). Roll out half of the dough into a circle about 11 inches (28 cm) in diameter. Transfer it to a 9-inch (23-cm) pie plate. Trim the overhang to 1 inch (2.5 cm) and refrigerate the crust.

Make the filling: In a large bowl, whisk together the sugar, cornstarch, ginger, cinnamon, and salt. Add the tomatoes, toss to coat, and transfer the mixture to the chilled bottom crust. Brush the rim of the crust with milk or egg wash.

Roll out the second half of the dough into a circle about 11 inches (28 cm) in diameter. Lay it over the filled pie plate and press the edges down to seal. Trim the overhang to 1 inch (2.5 cm), and tuck the top crust over the rim of the bottom crust. Crimp the edge into whatever pattern you like. Brush the top with egg wash or milk and sprinkle it with raw sugar.

Put the pie on a baking sheet and bake it for 20 minutes, rotating it once halfway through. Lower the temperature to 350°F (175°C) and bake it for 30 to 40 minutes more, until the crust is golden and the juices are thickened. Remove the pie to a rack to cool completely, at least 1 hour. This pie can be refrigerated for up to 1 week, covered in plastic wrap. Let it come to room temperature before serving, or warm it in a low oven. It can be kept frozen for up to 2 months: Wrap it in plastic, then in foil, and let it come to room temperature before serving.

GREEN TOMATO PIE

Yes, you read that right: Green Tomato Pie. Like avocados (whose pie can be found on page 82), tomatoes are a fruit in vegetable clothing. In their unripened, green state, they are very tart and can be used much like apples in dessert recipes. Once again, we have the South to thank for this delicious idea. Bake this one up, give it to a loved one, and see if they can guess what's inside!

MAKES one 9-inch (23-cm) pie

August

Here in New York City, August is brutal. It's an unholy marriage of heat and humidity, and those with the smarts and the means get out of town to somewhere with a body of water and a breeze. At this point in the summer, if I'm turning my oven on at all, it's for something really good. But if the idea of baking is completely unfathomable to you, I have got a few recipes here that require no oven at all!

....

TRIFECTA PIE
(CHOCOLATE-PEANUT BUTTER-PRETZEL)

When I started my pie business, I took some time to come up with flavors that really speak to my own tastes and preferences. While classic fruit and cream pies are delicious, what my palate craves is closer to a candy bar. I love the combination of super-salty pretzels, fluffy peanut butter mousse, and rich dark chocolate in this pie—it really is a flavor trifecta. As always, ingredients matter, so try to find rustic homestyle pretzels for your crust; I use Martin's pretzels, which are handmade in classic Pennsylvania Dutch style.

MAKES one 9-inch (23-cm) pie

PRETZEL CRUST
8 ounces (225 g) salted pretzels

6 to 8 tablespoons (85 to 115 g) unsalted butter, melted (pretzels can be very dry, so you may need more)

FILLING
3/4 cup (180 ml) heavy cream

4 ounces (115 g) cream cheese, at room temperature

1/2 cup (115 g) creamy peanut butter (if unsalted, add 1/4 teaspoon salt)

1/2 cup (50 g) powdered sugar

TOPPING
1/2 cup (137 g) bittersweet chocolate chips or pieces

1/4 cup (60 ml) heavy cream

Crumbled pretzel pieces, for garnish

Make the crust: Grind the pretzels in a food processor until finely ground or seal them in a plastic bag and crush them with a rolling pin. Pour in the butter and mix (hands are best for this) until the texture is that of wet sand. (You may need more or less butter, depending on the texture of the pretzels.) Firmly press the crumbs into a 9-inch (23-cm) pie pan (see page 50). Chill the crust in the freezer or fridge until ready to use.

Make the filling: In a stand mixer, with a hand mixer, or by hand with a whisk, whip the cream until stiff peaks form. Set the whipped cream aside.

Using the paddle attachment of the stand mixer (or a wooden spoon in a mixing bowl), mix together the cream cheese, peanut butter, and powdered sugar, starting at low speed and increasing the speed until the ingredients are fully incorporated. Scrape down the sides of the bowl, pour the whipped cream into the bowl, and mix again until all ingredients are fully blended.

Pour the peanut butter cream into the pretzel shell. Refrigerate it for 15 minutes to allow the cream to firm up.

Make the topping: Heat the cream over medium-high heat until it is scalded. Pour it over the chocolate pieces in a heatproof bowl. Allow it to stand for 1 minute, then whisk together to form a ganache. (You can also heat the cream and chocolate in the microwave at medium power for 1 minute, or in a double boiler.)

Pour the glaze over the peanut butter cream and spread it to the edges with a spatula. Decorate the top with pretzel pieces and refrigerate it for 15 minutes to firm the ganache. This pie can be refrigerated, covered in plastic wrap, for up to 1 week. It's also fantastic frozen, and can be stored in the freezer for up to 2 weeks.

TWO AUGUST PIES: Trifecta Pie
(pictured whole) and Banoffee
Pie (pictured sliced). See page
136 for Banoffee Pie recipe.

Graham Cracker Crust
(page 54) for one 9-inch
(23-cm) pie

FILLING

1 cup (240 ml) heavy cream

8 ounces (225 g) high-quality
milk chocolate, chopped
or chips

1 large egg, at room
temperature

1/4 teaspoon salt

TOPPING

1 tablespoon unflavored
gelatin

2 cups (400 g) sugar

2/3 cup (160 ml) light corn
syrup

1 teaspoon vanilla extract

S'MORES PIE

Preheat the oven to 350°F (175°C).

Make the filling: In a saucepan, heat the cream over medium-high heat until it is scalded. Pour it over the chocolate in a heatproof bowl and let it stand for 1 minute. Whisk it thoroughly until combined into a glossy ganache. Whisk in the egg and salt until fully incorporated.

Put the crust on a baking sheet. Pour the chocolate filling into the crust and bake it for 20 to 25 minutes, until the filling has just set and is still slightly wobbly in the center. Remove the pie to cool completely.

Make the topping: In the bowl of a stand mixer or in a large heatproof bowl, sprinkle the gelatin evenly over 2/3 cup (160 ml) water..

In a clean, heavy saucepan, combine the sugar, corn syrup, and another 2/3 cup (160 ml) water. Cook the sugar mixture over medium-high heat, stirring only at the beginning to dissolve the sugar, and boil it until a candy thermometer reaches the hard-ball stage (260°F/130°C). When the sugar is close to reaching this stage, turn on the stand mixer with the softened gelatin (or quickly beat the gelatin in your bowl to blend).

Once you've reached the right temperature, turn on the stand or hand mixer to low speed, and slowly pour the hot syrup in a steady stream into the gelatin while mixing. Try to avoid the sides of the bowl and aim for the space between the beater and the side. When all of the syrup is in, increase the speed gradually to high to avoid splashing, and continue to beat until the mixture is very thick and has tripled in volume, about 5 to 10 minutes. Add the vanilla, beat for a minute more, and then pour the topping over the pie. It will slowly spread to cover the surface, or you can use a spatula to spread it.

RECIPE CONTINUES

The first time I experimented with this recipe, I used a very dark, bittersweet chocolate (as a rule, I tend to prefer dark chocolate to milk chocolate). I can emphatically say that it was not a success. When you want to re-create the toasty, comforting taste of your childhood s'mores (always my favorite part of camping!), only milk chocolate will do. If you don't have the time, patience, or equipment necessary to make the marshmallow fluff (but try it; it's worth it!), you can place whole marshmallows over the cooled pie filling and toast those instead. It won't be as beautiful as the recipe below, but on what planet could toasted marshmallows be bad?

MAKES one 9-inch (23-cm) pie

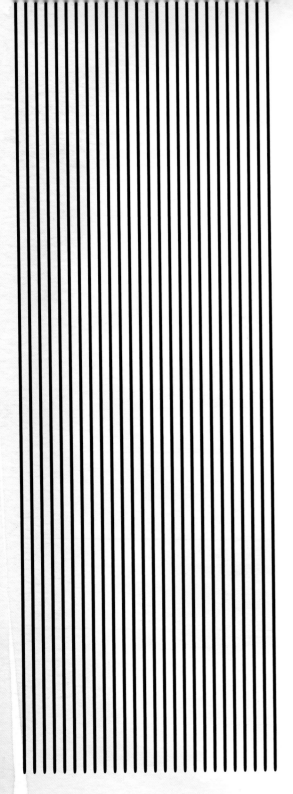

Allow the topping to cool at room temperature or in the fridge until it has set, about 30 minutes. If you are using a torch (the preferred method), make sure the area you are working in is clear of any plastic, paper, or other flammable items, and that the surface you are working on is fireproof (steel, marble, etc.). You can put a baking sheet under the pie to protect your countertops. Light the torch and start to lightly toast the surface of the pie, going darker or lighter according to your preference (I like my marshmallow pretty scorched, but that's me!). When the pie is perfectly brûléed, turn off the torch, and allow the pie to cool for 10 minutes.

If you are torch-less, you can do this in the broiler, but keep a close eye, as it requires patience, watchfulness, and speed. Preheat your broiler, put the pie on a baking sheet, and use foil or a pie shield to cover the crust edges. Broil the pie about 3 inches (7.5 cm) from the heat source, rotating the pie for even toasting, until the topping is at your desired color. It burns very easily with this method, so watch closely! It's best to keep the oven door cracked open and watch and rotate the whole time. Remove the pie and allow it to cool for at least 10 minutes.

Your pie is now ready to serve, or you can keep it in the fridge for up to 1 week. To cover, spray foil or plastic wrap very lightly with oil spray to prevent it from sticking to the topping. For easier slicing, run your knife under hot water first to prevent the marshmallow from sticking to the blade.

1. Pour hot cream over the chocolate; let it stand for one minute.

2. Whisk the cream and melted chocolate into a glossy ganache.

3. Whisk in a single egg and a pinch of salt.

4. Pour the filling into your Graham Cracker Crust.

1. Pour ⅔ cup of water . . .

2. Add two cups of sugar . . .

5. Beat into a bloomed gelatin mixture until it's thick and fluffy.

6. Mix in vanilla.

3. And ⅔ cup of corn syrup into a saucepan. Stir to combine.

4. Cook over high heat until the hard ball stage.

7. Pour marshmallow fluff topping over the pie.

8. Torch it up!

BANOFFEE PIE

I had the great pleasure of living in London for awhile, and the British version of banana cream pie quickly became my favorite. With its layers of sweet, gooey dulce de leche, fresh bananas, and sugarless whipped cream, it's perfectly balanced—rich and light at the same time. If you can't find British digestive biscuits at your local market, specialty stores should carry them, or you can substitute whole-wheat or graham crackers. You can see what Banoffee Pie looks like on page 129.

MAKES one 9-inch (23-cm) pie

FILLING

1 (14-ounce/400-g) can sweetened condensed milk (organic preferred; get one that's only milk and sugar if possible)

3 large medium-ripe bananas

CRUST

1 (10-ounce/280-g) package digestive biscuits (McVitie's and Carr's Whole Wheat are good brands)

5 to 8 tablespoons (70 to 115 g) unsalted butter, melted

TOPPING

1½ cups (360 ml) heavy cream

Shaved dark chocolate (optional)

Make the filling: In a very large, deep pot, boil the can of sweetened condensed milk, unopened, for 4 hours. It's best to do a few cans together so you'll have dulce de leche on hand for other recipes. It is crucial that the cans remain submerged in water the entire time, or they may explode. Turn off the heat and let them cool completely in the water before using.

Make the crust: Grind the biscuits in a food processor until finely ground or seal them in a plastic bag and crush them with a rolling pin. Pour in the butter and mix (hands are best for this) until the texture is that of wet sand. Firmly press the crumbs into a 9-inch (23-cm) pie pan (see page 50). Chill the crust in the freezer or fridge.

Spread the dulce de leche into the bottom of the crust.

Slice the bananas into circles or lengthwise into strips. Arrange them over the caramel.

Make the topping: In a stand mixer, with a hand mixer, or by hand with a whisk, whip the cream until stiff peaks form. Pile it on top of the bananas and sprinkle with shaved chocolate, if using. Slice the pie and serve. This pie is best made right before serving. You can store it, covered in plastic wrap, in the refrigerator, but be warned that the bananas will brown.

Classic Pie Crust (page 38)
  for one 9-inch (23-cm) pie

FILLING

6 cups (900 g) cubed seedless
  watermelon

¹/₄ cup (30 g) cornstarch

¹/₂ cup (100 g) granulated
  sugar

¹/₄ cup (60 ml) freshly
  squeezed lime juice

¹/₄ teaspoon salt

TOPPING

1 cup (240 ml) heavy cream

2 tablespoons powdered sugar

¹/₂ teaspoon vanilla extract

WATERMELON CREAM PIE

It's hard to get enough fresh
watermelon in the summer, but when
those big green orbs are in such
abundance, I like to find new ways
to use them other than just slicing
and eating. I use them in salads
with salty cheese, in cocktails
with tequila and lime, and in this
pie, with a hefty dollop of whipped
cream. It's so refreshing, light,
and unique!

MAKES one 9-inch (23-cm) pie

Preheat the oven to 425°F (220°C). Roll out the dough into a circle about 11 inches (28 cm) in diameter. Transfer it to a 9-inch (23-cm) pie plate, trim the overhang to about 1 inch (2.5 cm), tuck the overhang under, and crimp decoratively. Blind-bake the pie crust until it is fully baked (see page 35); set it aside to cool.

Make the filling: In a blender, puree the watermelon chunks until smooth. Strain the puree through a fine-mesh sieve into a large saucepan, pushing on the solids to extract all the juice. Discard the solids. You should have about 4 cups (960 ml) of strained puree. If you have extra, use it for cocktails, popsicles, or drink it fresh! Ladle out about ¼ cup (60 ml) of the puree into a small bowl, whisk in the cornstarch, and set aside.

Add the granulated sugar, lime juice, and salt to the remaining puree in the pan, and bring it to a boil, whisking frequently. When the juice is boiling, stir the cornstarch mixture again to make sure it's completely smooth, and then whisk it into the boiling pot. Simmer for about 5 minutes, whisking constantly, until the filling has thickened to coat the back of a spoon.

Put the pie crust on a baking sheet. Pour the filling into the crust, smoothing the surface with a spatula. Refrigerate it, uncovered, for about 1 hour, then cover it with plastic wrap and refrigerate it for at least 4 hours or overnight.

Make the topping: In a stand mixer, with a hand mixer, or by hand with a whisk, whip the cream, sugar, and vanilla until stiff peaks form. Spread the whipped cream over the filling, slice the pie, and serve. This pie can be made ahead, without the topping, and refrigerated for up to 3 days, covered in plastic wrap. Add the whipped cream topping right before serving.

ROOT BEER FLOAT PIE

I am not a big soda drinker, but man, do I love a good root beer. The combination of spicy, creamy, and herbal flavors really gets me going, and when you plunk a big scoop of vanilla ice cream in there, well, that's pretty much heaven. I set out to make a pie version of this soda-fountain classic and, after much trial and error, I arrived at this recipe. Use your favorite root beer and good-quality vanilla.

MAKES one 9-inch (23-cm) pie

2 cups (480 ml) root beer

Gingersnap and Vanilla Wafer Crust, made from equal parts of each type of cookie (see pages 52 and 66 for recipes, or use store-bought cookies) for one 9-inch (23-cm) pie

FILLING

3 large eggs, lightly beaten

1/2 cup (100 g) firmly packed dark brown sugar

1/4 teaspoon salt

TOPPING

1 cup (240 ml) heavy cream

2 tablespoons sugar

1 teaspoon pure vanilla extract

Make root beer syrup by boiling the root beer in a medium pot until it is reduced by half, leaving you with 1 cup (240 ml) of liquid. Allow it to cool completely.

Make the crust: Grind the cookies in a food processor until finely ground, or seal them in a plastic bag and crush them with a rolling pin. Pour in the butter and mix (hands are best for this) until the texture is that of wet sand. Firmly press the crumbs into a 9-inch (23-cm) pie pan (see page 50). Chill the crust in the freezer or fridge while preheating the oven to 350°F (175°C). Bake the crust for 10 minutes, and then let it cool completely. Leave the oven on.

Make the filling: In a large bowl, whisk together the eggs, brown sugar, and salt, then whisk in the root beer syrup until fully incorporated.

Put the pie crust on a baking sheet. Pour the filling into the crust and bake it for 20 to 25 minutes, until the filling has just set and is still slightly wobbly in the center. Remove the pie to a rack to cool completely.

Make the topping: In a stand mixer, with a hand mixer, or by hand with a whisk, whip the cream, sugar, and vanilla together until soft peaks form. Pile the whipped cream on top of the cooled pie and refrigerate it for at least 30 minutes. This pie can be made, without the topping, and refrigerated, covered in plastic wrap, for up to 1 week. Top with whipped cream just before serving.

Classic Pie (page 38) or
    Cornmeal Crust (page 44)
    for one double-crust
    9-inch (23-cm) pie

FILLING

2 pounds (910 g) ripe
    freestone peaches,
    peeled, pitted, and
    sliced (see Note)

1 teaspoon grated peeled
    fresh ginger

1 teaspoon ground ginger

1/2 cup (110 g) firmly packed
    dark brown sugar

1/4 cup (30 g) cornstarch

1/4 teaspoon salt

Egg wash (page 25) or milk,
    for glaze

Raw sugar, for garnish

GINGER-PEACH PIE

Preheat the oven to 425°F (220°C). On a clean, lightly floured surface, roll out half of the dough into an 11-inch (28-cm) circle about ⅛ to ¼ inch (3 to 6 mm) thick. Line a 9-inch (23-cm) pie plate with the dough, and trim the overhang to about 1 inch (2.5 cm). Refrigerate the crust until ready to bake.

Make the filling: In a large bowl, toss together the peaches and both kinds of ginger. In a separate bowl, mix together the sugar, cornstarch, and salt. Just before adding the filling to the pie plate, toss the fruit in the dry ingredients. Brush the rim of the bottom crust with egg wash or milk.

Roll out the second half of the dough into an 11-inch (28-cm) circle and lay it over the filled pie. Trim the edges, and tuck the top crust over the rim of the bottom crust to form a tight seal. Crimp the edge into whatever pattern you like. Brush the top crust with egg wash or milk, sprinkle it with raw sugar, and cut a few slits to allow steam to escape.

Put the pie on a baking sheet and bake it for 20 minutes, turning the pie once halfway through. Lower the temperature to 350°F (175°C) and bake the pie for 30 to 40 minutes more, until the crust is golden and fully baked and the juices have thickened. Remove it to a rack to cool completely, at least 1 hour.

This pie can be refrigerated for up to 1 week, covered in plastic wrap. Let it come to room temperature before serving, or warm it in a low oven. It can be kept frozen for up to 2 months: Wrap it in plastic, then in foil, and let it come to room temperature before serving.

NOTE To easily peel peaches, prepare an ice bath in a large bowl. Bring a pot of water to a boil. Lightly score the skin of the peaches with an "x" on the bottom, blanch each one in the boiling water for about 30 seconds, and transfer to the ice bath. The skins should slip right off the fruit with the help of a paring knife. If they don't peel easily, repeat the process until they do.

Do you need to add anything to ripe peaches? Absolutely not. But it certainly doesn't hurt to toss in some fresh ginger, which gives a little spicy, warm kick to those sweet, juicy peaches. Add it or leave it out; you'll love this pie either way. I prefer to use freestone peaches, which describes those with pits that separate easily from the fruit. Clingstone peaches will more tenaciously hold on to their pits, making them more difficult to work with.

MAKES one 9-inch (23-cm) pie

SUGAR PLUM PIE

|||||||||||||||||||||||||||||||

When I was a little girl, I got to go see my cousin Daniel perform in the Joffrey Ballet's annual staging of *The Nutcracker* in New York City. I was completely obsessed by the story, Daniel's beautiful dancing as the Snow King, and, of course, the incredible music. "The Dance of the Sugar Plum Fairy" was always my favorite scene. Traditionally, sugar plums were candies made of a variety of dried fruits chopped up and combined with sugar and spices. This pie goes the fresh route, using in-season plums, with honey and some cardamom. I like to use a mix of damson, black, red, and yellow plums, but go with whatever is in season. I hope it will inspire you to do a little dance yourself!

MAKES one 9-inch (23-cm) pie

Classic Pie (page 38) or
Cornmeal Crust (page 44)
for one double-crust
9-inch (23-cm) pie

FILLING

2 to 3 pounds (910 g to 1.4 kg) ripe plums, pitted, peeled, and sliced (see Note, page 139)

1/4 cup (60 ml) wildflower honey (or other fragrant variety)

1/2 teaspoon vanilla extract

1/2 cup (110 g) firmly packed dark brown sugar

1/4 cup (30 g) cornstarch

1/4 teaspoon salt

1/8 teaspoon ground cardamom (optional)

Egg wash (page 25) or milk, for glaze

Raw sugar, for garnish

Preheat the oven to 425°F (220°C). On a clean, lightly floured surface, roll out half of the dough into an 11-inch (28-cm) circle about 1/8 to 1/4 inch (3 to 6 mm) thick. Line a 9-inch (23-cm) pie plate with the dough, and trim the overhang to about 1 inch (2.5 cm). Refrigerate the crust until ready to bake.

Make the filling: In a large bowl, toss together the plums, honey, and vanilla. In a separate bowl, mix together the sugar, cornstarch, salt, and cardamom, if using. Just before adding the filling to the pie plate, toss the fruit in the dry ingredients. Brush the rim of the bottom crust with egg wash or milk.

Roll out the second half of the dough into a circle about 11 inches (28 cm) in diameter. Cut it into lattice strips or decorative shapes with a cookie cutter (see page 30) and arrange them over the filling. Trim the overhang, roll the dough under, and press it to seal. Crimp the edge into whatever pattern you like, brush the crust with egg wash or milk, and sprinkle raw sugar over the top.

Put the pie on a baking sheet and bake it for 20 minutes, turning the pie once halfway through. Lower the temperature to 350°F (175°C) and bake the pie for 30 to 40 minutes more, until the crust is golden and fully baked and the juices have thickened. Remove the pie to a rack to cool completely, at least 1 hour. This pie can be refrigerated for up to 1 week, covered in plastic wrap. Let it come to room temperature before serving, or warm it in a low oven. It can be kept frozen for up to 2 months: Wrap it in plastic, then in foil, and let it come to room temperature before serving.

1. Lightly score an "x" on the bottom of each plum.

2. Blanch scored plums in boiling water for 30 seconds.

3. Immerse plums in an ice bath, and peel off the skins.

4. Slice the plums, toss with dry ingredients, and pile into your pie crust.

September

In a sense, September feels like the beginning of the year. People go back to school, back to work, back to real life, and we start to hunker down and cook more meals at home. The craving for comfort foods and homemade treats becomes stronger, and all of those apples rolling off the tree just beg to be baked into pies.

CANDY APPLE PIE

This pie took the Judge's Prize at Just Food's 2012 "Let Us Eat Local" pie contest in New York City (said judges were Melissa Clark, Johnny Iuzzini, Ed Levine, and Josh Ozersky—a pretty intimidating bunch!). The challenge was to create something seasonal, using as many local ingredients as possible, and of course to make it delicious. As usual, my boyfriend, Jay, furnished the brilliant idea: a riff on those bright-red, tooth-cracking carnival candy apples of our youth. With its tart apple-cider caramel filling and drizzle of spicy, crunchy candy, I think you'll agree with the judges—this pie is a winner!

I slice the apples very thinly for my pies so they bake through nicely in the oven. If you prefer a chunkier apple, you'll need to cook your filling on the stove over medium heat for a few minutes until the apples have softened, before filling your pie. Nobody likes a raw apple pie!

MAKES one 9-inch (23-cm) pie

Classic Pie Crust (page 38) for one double-crust 9-inch (23-cm) pie

FILLING

2 cups (480 ml) apple cider

1/2 cup (1 stick/115 g) unsalted butter

3/4 cup (165 g) firmly packed dark brown sugar

3/4 cup (180 ml) heavy cream

1/2 teaspoon ground ginger

1/2 teaspoon cinnamon

1/2 teaspoon sea salt

2 pounds (910 g) tart apples, peeled and thinly sliced

Egg wash (page 25) or milk, for glaze

Raw sugar, for garnish

CANDY TOPPING

1 cup (200 g) granulated sugar

2/3 cup (165 ml) light corn syrup

1/2 teaspoon cayenne (or more to taste)

1/2 teaspoon cinnamon

10 to 15 drops red food coloring

Preheat the oven to 425°F (220°C). Roll out half of the dough into a circle about 11 inches (28 cm) in diameter. Transfer it to a 9-inch (23-cm) pie plate. Trim the overhang to 1 inch (2.5 cm) and refrigerate the crust.

Make the filling: In a heavy-bottomed saucepan over high heat, cook the cider until it's reduced down to ½ cup (120 ml). Lower the heat to medium-high, melt the butter in the cider syrup, then whisk in the brown sugar, cream, ginger, cinnamon, and salt. Bring the mixture to a gentle boil and cook for 7 to 10 minutes, until it is dark, thick, and glossy. Remove it from the heat and allow it to cool to just warm.

Layer the apple slices in the pie plate, and pour the caramel sauce over. Brush the pie shell edges with egg wash, milk, or extra cream.

Roll out the second half of the dough into a circle about 11 inches (28 cm) in diameter. Lay it over the filled pie plate, and press the edges down to seal. Trim the overhang to 1 inch (2.5 cm), and roll the edges of the dough inward or outward. Crimp the edge into whatever pattern you like, and brush the top with egg wash or milk.

RECIPE CONTINUES

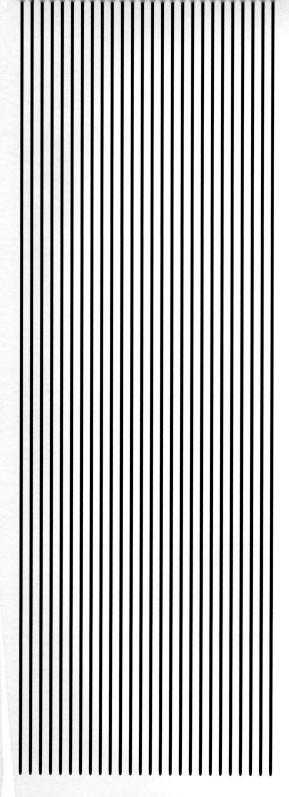

Put the pie on a baking sheet and bake it for 20 minutes, rotating it once halfway through. Lower the temperature to 350°F (175°C) and bake it for 30 to 40 minutes more, until the crust is golden and the juices are thickened. Remove it to a wire rack to cool completely, at least 1 hour.

Make the topping: In a heavy-bottomed saucepan, heat the granulated sugar, corn syrup, and ⅓ cup (75 ml) water over high heat. Cook until the syrup reaches 300°F (150°C) on a candy thermometer. Remove the pan from the heat and whisk in the cayenne, cinnamon, and food coloring (be careful, it will bubble up and release a lot of steam). Using a fork, drizzle the hot candy over the top of the pie in circles, or whatever pattern pleases you. Do this immediately to prevent the candy from hardening too quickly. If it becomes difficult to use, heat it gently over low heat to soften it again.

This pie is best served shortly after it's been baked, and leftovers should be kept boxed in a cardboard or plastic container at room temperature. The condensation in the refrigerator will soften the candy topping, and you'll lose that delightful crunch.

Classic Pie Crust (page 38)
    for one 9-inch (23-cm) pie

FILLING

5 cups (1.2 L) whole milk

6 tablespoons (45 g)
    cornstarch

4 large eggs

$^{1}/_{2}$ cup (1 stick/115 g)
    unsalted butter

2 cups (440 g) firmly packed
    dark brown sugar

1 teaspoon sea salt

2 tablespoons Scotch whisky

1 teaspoon vanilla extract

TOPPING

1 cup (240 ml) heavy cream

2 tablespoons powdered sugar

1 tablespoon Scotch whisky

BUTTERSCOTCH CREAM PIE

As I am co-owner of a dessert bar called Butter & Scotch, it's pretty clear I love butterscotch. I love it even more when there's a splash of real Scotch whisky mixed in! I recommend using a good Scotch that you'd be happy to drink, but steer clear of the super-smoky Islay malts for this one. My personal choice would be Johnnie Walker Black.

MAKES one 9-inch (23-cm) pie

Preheat the oven to 425°F (220°C). Roll out the dough into a circle about 11 inches (28 cm) in diameter. Transfer it to a 9-inch (23-cm) pie plate, trim the overhang to about 1 inch (2.5 cm), tuck the overhang under, and crimp decoratively. Blind-bake the pie crust until it is fully baked (see page 35); set it aside to cool.

Make the filling: In a small bowl, whisk together ½ cup (120 ml) of the milk and the cornstarch. Once they are fully combined, whisk in the eggs and set aside.

In a large saucepan over medium-high heat, melt the butter. Mix in the brown sugar and salt and cook until the sugar has melted. It will turn a dark amber color and you'll smell the caramelized sugar. Remove the pan from the heat and allow the caramel to cool slightly, about 10 minutes.

Whisk the remaining milk into the butter-and-sugar mixture (the sugar will seize up a bit; don't worry, it will melt again). Whisk in the cornstarch-egg mixture. Return the pan to medium-high heat and bring it to a boil, whisking frequently. Once it begins to boil, lower the heat to a simmer, and whisk constantly until the pudding has thickened and coats the back of a wooden spoon.

Remove it from the heat, whisk in the Scotch and vanilla, and pour the filling into the pie shell. Refrigerate it, with plastic wrap pressed to the surface of the pudding, until the filling is fully chilled and set, 3 to 4 hours.

Make the topping: In a stand mixer, with a hand mixer, or by hand with a whisk, whip the cream, powdered sugar, and Scotch until stiff peaks form. Spread the whipped cream over the filling, slice the pie, and serve. This pie can be made ahead and stored for up to 1 week, without the topping, and refrigerated covered in plastic wrap (make sure the plastic touches the surface of the filling). Make the topping just before serving.

Classic Pie Crust (page 38) for one 9-inch (23-cm) pie

FILLING

1 tablespoon unflavored gelatin

2/3 cup (130 g) sugar

3 large eggs, separated

1/4 teaspoon salt

5 tablespoons (75 ml) good rye whiskey (bourbon works beautifully as well)

1 1/2 tablespoons sweet vermouth (I recommend Carpano or Vya)

1 1/2 tablespoons dry vermouth

5 dashes Angostura or orange bitters

1 cup (240 ml) heavy cream

Brandied cherries and/or chopped lemon rind, for garnish (optional)

PERFECT MANHATTAN PIE

Preheat the oven to 425°F (220°C). Roll out the dough into a circle about 11 inches (28 cm) in diameter. Transfer it to a 9-inch (23-cm) pie plate, trim the overhang to about 1 inch (2.5 cm), tuck the overhang under, and crimp decoratively. Blind-bake the pie crust until it is fully baked (see page 35); set it aside to cool.

Make the filling: Pour 1/2 cup (120 ml) cold water in a heavy-bottomed saucepan and evenly dust it with the gelatin. Allow the mixture to bloom, about 5 minutes.

Whisk 1/3 cup (65 g) of the sugar, the egg yolks, and salt into the gelatin mixture. Stir it over low heat until the gelatin dissolves and the mixture thickens to just coat the back of a spoon. Remove it from the heat.

Stir the whiskey, vermouths, and bitters into the mixture and refrigerate it, uncovered, until it begins to firm up and mound slightly when pushed with a spoon, about 30 minutes. If you let the mixture chill for too long, and it sets up too firmly, just warm it gently over low heat, whisking constantly, and then refrigerate again until it sets properly.

In a stand mixer or mixing bowl, beat the egg whites until soft peaks form, then add the remaining 1/3 cup (65 g) sugar and beat until you have a stiff meringue. Fold the meringue into the custard mixture.

In a stand mixer, with a hand mixer, or by hand with a whisk, whip the cream, then gently fold it into the filling. Spread the filling into the crust and garnish it with the cherries and/or lemon rind, if desired. Refrigerate the pie completely, loosely covered in plastic wrap, or in a cardboard or plastic container, for at least 4 hours or overnight. This pie can be kept refrigerated for up to 1 week.

As a partner in a dessert and cocktail bar, and a former bartender to boot, I just had to include a pie inspired by my favorite cocktail. A "Perfect Manhattan" is just that: a perfectly balanced cocktail, with equal amounts of sweet and dry vermouth to keep it from being cloying. Based on a classic 1970s recipe published in the *New York Times*, this chiffon pie is endlessly adaptable, and you can use it as a formula to whip up whatever cocktail-themed pie you desire (though a Dirty Martini might not work so well). Keep the booze to 1/2 cup (120 ml), and you'll be good to go (and feeling woozy!).

Adapted from "Dick Taeuber's Cordial Pie" by Craig Claiborne in the *New York Times*.

MAKES one 9-inch (23-cm) pie

SPICED FIG PIE

Figs are among my favorite fall fruits. They are gorgeous to look at, and they have a fresh sweetness that makes it hard to eat just one. They become even more beautiful when roasted or when baked in this pie. I've accented their delicious flavor with some honey and spices, and given you a range of crust options, from the buttery to the chocolatey. They all taste delightful.

MAKES   one 9-inch (23-cm) pie

Classic Pie (page 38), Cornmeal (page 44), or Chocolate Pie Crust (page 47) for one 9-inch (23-cm) pie

FILLING

1 pound (455 g) fresh figs (Mission or Turkish figs are great) (about 9 to 12 pieces), sliced in half lengthwise and stemmed

1 star anise pod

3 whole cloves

$1/2$ cup (120 ml) honey (a nice dark one is good for this recipe)

$1/4$ cup (55 g) firmly packed dark brown sugar

$1/4$ cup ($1/2$ stick/55 g) unsalted butter, melted

2 tablespoons cornstarch

$1/8$ teaspoon ground allspice

$1/4$ teaspoon salt

TOPPING

Lemon zest (optional)

Preheat the oven to 425°F (220°C). Roll out the dough into a circle about 11 inches (28 cm) in diameter. Transfer it to a 9-inch (23-cm) pie plate, trim the overhang to about 1 inch (2.5 cm), tuck the overhang under, and crimp decoratively. Blind-bake the pie crust until partially baked (see page 35); set it aside to cool. Lower the oven to 350°F (175ºC).

Make the filling: Arrange the figs, cut side up, in the bottom of the pie crust, keeping them pressed closely together.

In a spice grinder, coffee mill, or mortar and pestle, finely grind the star anise and cloves.

In a large bowl, whisk together the honey, sugar, butter, cornstarch, allspice, and salt until combined. Pour the mixture over the figs.

Put the pie on a baking sheet and bake it for 30 to 50 minutes, until the figs are tender and the juices are thickened. Remove it to a rack to cool completely, at least 1 hour. Sprinkle with lemon zest, if using. This pie can be kept refrigerated, covered in plastic wrap, for up to 5 days. Allow it to come to room temperature, or warm it through in a low oven, before serving.

PERSIMMON PIE

Every year in late fall, persimmons magically appear in my local Asian market. Those glossy, deep-orange globes are heavenly to eat with nothing other than a spoon, but this pie is an exciting option as well. Many persimmon pies wind up tasting like pumpkin pies, with all the spices added. I left those out, opting for just a splash of vanilla and lemon juice, so you can really taste the fruit.

You will likely find two types of persimmons at the market: Fuyu and Hachiya. Fuyus are rounder, and can be eaten crisp, like an apple. Hachiyas are more heart-shaped, and must be eaten only when extremely ripe: They should feel like a water balloon and have thin, translucent skin. Underripe Hachiyas = a puckery mouth. Whichever type you use for this recipe, you'll want them to be nice and soft.

MAKES one 9-inch (23-cm) pie

Classic Pie Crust (page 38) for one 9-inch (23-cm) pie

FILLING

1 pound (455 g) very ripe persimmons

1/2 cup (110 g) firmly packed light brown sugar

3 large eggs

2 tablespoons unsalted butter, melted

1 teaspoon freshly squeezed lemon juice

1/2 teaspoon vanilla extract

1/4 teaspoon salt

1 cup (240 ml) heavy cream

Whipped cream or ice cream (optional)

Preheat the oven to 425°F (220°C). Roll out the dough into a circle about 11 inches (28 cm) in diameter. Transfer it to a 9-inch (23-cm) pie plate, trim the overhang to about 1 inch (2.5 cm), tuck the overhang under, and crimp decoratively. Blind-bake the pie crust until partially baked (see page 35); set it aside to cool. Lower the oven to 350°F (175°C).

Make the filling: Use a food mill with a fine blade to process the persimmons. If you don't have a food mill, remove the calyx (the dried leaves on the top of the fruit) and seeds, and process the fruit in a food processor, or push it through a medium-mesh sieve, discarding the solids. You should have about 1½ cups (360 ml) of puree.

In a food processor, blender, or by hand, combine the sugar and eggs, then blend in the persimmon puree, butter, lemon juice, vanilla, and salt. Finish by adding the cream.

Put the pie crust on a baking sheet. Pour the filling into the crust and bake it for 45 minutes to 1 hour, until the pie is just set and still slightly wobbly in the center. Remove the pie to a rack to cool completely, at least 1 hour. Serve slices with whipped cream or ice cream, if desired. This pie can be refrigerated for up to 1 week, covered in plastic wrap.

Classic Pie Crust (page 38) for one double-crust 9-inch (23-cm) pie

FILLING

2 to 3 pounds (910 g to 1.4 kg) ripe or slightly crisp pears, unpeeled, cored, and thinly sliced

1/2 cup (120 ml) clover honey

2 tablespoons roughly chopped fresh tarragon

2 tablespoons absinthe or Pernod

2 tablespoons cornstarch

1/4 teaspoon salt

Egg wash (page 25) or milk, for glaze

Raw sugar, for garnish

Preheat the oven to 425°F (220°C). On a clean, lightly floured surface, roll out half of the dough into an 11-inch (28-cm) circle about ⅛ to ¼ inch (3 to 6 mm) thick. Line a 9-inch (23-cm) pie plate with the dough, and trim the overhang to about 1 inch (2.5 cm). Refrigerate the crust until ready to bake.

Make the filling: In a large bowl, toss together the pears, honey, tarragon, absinthe or Pernod, cornstarch, and salt. Pile the filling into the pie plate, and brush the exposed edge of the pie crust with egg wash or milk.

Roll out the second half of the dough into an 11-inch (28-cm) circle. Lay it over the filled pie. Trim the edges, and tuck the top crust over the rim of the bottom crust to form a tight seal. Crimp the edge into whatever pattern you like. Brush the top crust with egg wash or milk, sprinkle it with raw sugar, and cut a few slits to allow steam to escape.

Put the pie on a baking sheet and bake it for 20 minutes, turning the pie once halfway through. Lower the temperature to 350°F (175°C) and bake it for 30 to 40 minutes more, until the crust is golden and fully baked and the juices have thickened. Remove it to a wire rack to cool completely, at least 1 hour. This pie can be refrigerated for up to 1 week, covered in plastic wrap. Let it come to room temperature before serving, or warm it in a low oven. It can be kept frozen for up to 2 months: Cover it in plastic wrap, then in foil, and let it come to room temperature before serving.

HONEY-PEAR PIE

Summer always gets all of the seasonal-fruit cred, but fall has some stellar offerings. I'm always very happy to see those first pears at the farmers' market, as it signals an impending avalanche of different varieties: Bosc, Bartlett, Starkrimson, Anjou, Seckel ... I love 'em all. Of course I'll happily munch some fresh pear slices alongside a nice wedge of cheese, but this pie is one of my absolute favorite ways to use these fragrant, delicate fruits. The honey, tarragon, and absinthe in this recipe might seem surprising, but they meld perfectly with the sweet fragrance of autumn pears.

MAKES one 9-inch (23-cm) pie

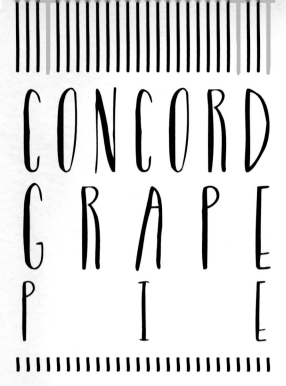

CONCORD GRAPE PIE

I'm not going to lie to you: This pie is labor-intensive. But man, is it worth the work! I just love it when fall rolls around with its abundance of dark purple, intensely perfumed Concord and Niagara grapes. These grapes, which are indigenous to North America, are very different from their European cousins. Their firm, thick skins encase sweet, translucent flesh and some serious seeds. They are so fragrant and have a pure, pronounced grape flavor. I was inspired by a cocktail served at Cookshop restaurant in New York, and added in some rosemary, which complements the grapes elegantly.

MAKES one 9-inch (23-cm) pie

FILLING

2 pounds (910 g) Concord grapes, stemmed and rinsed

2 fresh rosemary sprigs

1/2 cup (100 g) sugar

1/2 cup (60 g) cornstarch

1/4 teaspoon salt

2 tablespoons gin (optional)

Egg wash (page 25) or milk, for glaze

Raw sugar, for garnish

Classic Pie (page 38) or Cornmeal Crust (page 44) for one double-crust 9-inch (23-cm) pie

To prepare the grapes, place a sieve or colander inside a large bowl. Using your fingers, pinch the flesh of the grapes out of the skins; they should pop right out into the sieve. Repeat this process for all of the grapes, and reserve the skins in a large heatproof bowl. I recommend doing this in front of a good movie! Drink the juice that strains into the bowl, or save it for making jelly or cocktails.

Make the filling: Pour the flesh into a heavy-bottomed saucepan. Toss the rosemary into the saucepan, and boil the grapes over medium-high heat for about 5 minutes, stirring occasionally, until they soften and start to fall apart. The seeds will separate from the pulp of the grapes, making it easier to strain. Remove and discard the rosemary sprigs.

Pour the pulp mixture into a medium sieve over the bowl of grape skins. Using a spatula or wooden spoon, press and stir the flesh through the sieve until all of the juices are in the bowl. Discard the solids.

Preheat the oven to 425°F (220°C). On a clean, lightly floured surface, roll out half of the dough into an 11-inch (28-cm) circle about 1/8 to 1/4 inch (3 to 6 mm) thick. Line a 9-inch (23-cm) pie plate with the dough, and trim the overhang to about 1 inch (2.5 cm). Refrigerate the crust until ready to bake.

In a blender or food processor, puree the grape skins and juices. Add the sugar, cornstarch, salt, and gin (if using) and process until blended. Put the pie crust on a baking sheet and pour in the grape filling.

Roll out the second half of the dough into a 6-inch (15-cm) circle (you will have extra dough to use for something else). Lay this in the center of the filling, so there is a circle of grape filling showing around the edge. Alternatively, you can use cookie cutters (grape-leaf shapes are an excellent choice) to cut the dough and arrange it over the top of the filling. It's nice to see some of the grape showing through; it's a beautiful color.

Brush the crust with egg wash or milk, sprinkle it with some raw sugar, and bake the pie for 20 minutes, rotating it once halfway through.

Lower the temperature to 350°F (175°C) and bake the pie for 45 minutes more, or until the juices have thickened and the crust is golden. Remove it to a rack to cool completely, at least 2 hours. This pie can be refrigerated for up to 1 week, covered in plastic wrap. Allow it to come to room temperature before serving.

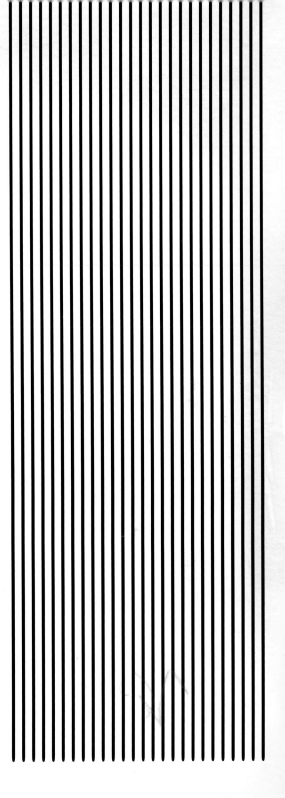

October

Of all the months in the year, I'm partial to October. Perhaps it's because it's my birthday month (that's probably why), perhaps it's because it's the month of my favorite holiday (Halloween, duh!), or perhaps it has something to do with the apples and the pumpkins and the cider and the leaves. Whatever it is, this is my happiest time of the year.

APPLE-CHEDDAR PIE

Once upon a time, in diners and roadside joints all across America, it wasn't unusual to sit down to a warm slice of apple pie with a hunk of Cheddar cheese melting on top. Somehow, this fine tradition has been forgotten in most places, but I'm here to do my part to resurrect it. Nothing heightens and brightens the tart, sweet flavor of apple pie like a sharp, salty slice of Cheddar. In my recipe, I like to melt the cheese on top of the crust toward the end of the baking time, so it gets nice and toasty. You'll never want to eat plain old apple pie again.

MAKES   one 9-inch (23-cm) pie

Classic Pie Crust (page 38) for one double-crust 9-inch (23-cm) pie (see Note)

FILLING
1/2 cup (110 g) firmly packed brown sugar

1/2 teaspoon ground ginger

1/2 teaspoon cinnamon

1/4 teaspoon salt

2 to 3 pounds (910 g to 1.4 kg) large tart apples (Granny Smith, Rome, Mcintosh, Macoun, and Cortland are all good)

Egg wash (page 25) or milk, for glaze

Raw sugar, for garnish

TOPPING
1/2 cup (60 g) shredded extra-sharp Cheddar cheese

Preheat the oven to 425°F (220°C). On a clean, lightly floured surface, roll out half of the dough into an 11-inch (28-cm) circle about ⅛ to ¼ inch (3 to 6 mm) thick. Line a 9-inch (23-cm) pie plate with the dough, and trim the overhang to about 1 inch (2.5 cm). Refrigerate the crust until ready to bake.

Make the filling: In a large bowl, whisk together the brown sugar, ginger, cinnamon, and salt. Add the apples and toss to coat.

Fill the chilled crust with the apple mixture and brush the edges with egg wash or milk. Roll out the second half of the dough and lay it over the filling. Trim the edges, roll the dough under, and press to seal. Crimp the edge into a decorative pattern, brush the crust with egg wash or milk, and sprinkle raw sugar over the top. Cut vents into the top crust to allow steam to escape during baking.

Put the pie on a baking sheet and bake it for 20 minutes, rotating it once halfway through. Lower the temperature to 350°F (175°C) and bake it for another 20 minutes, then pull out the pie and sprinkle the Cheddar all over the top crust. Bake the pie for 10 to 20 minutes more, until the crust is golden, the Cheddar is melted and browning, and the juices are thickened. Remove the pie to a wire rack to cool completely, at least 1 hour.

This pie can be refrigerated for up to 1 week, covered in plastic wrap. Let it come to room temperature before serving, or warm it in a low oven. It can be kept frozen for up to 2 months: Cover it in plastic wrap, then in foil, and let it come to room temperature before serving.

NOTE To make this pie extra-cheesy, add ¼ cup (30 g) shredded sharp Cheddar to the pie dough. To do this, cut it in at the same time as the butter when making the dough by hand, or pulse it in with the butter if making it in the food processor.

FILLING

1/4 cup (1/2 stick/55 g) unsalted butter, melted, plus extra butter for greasing the dish

2 to 3 pounds (910 g to 1.4 kg) large tart apples (Granny Smith, Rome, Mcintosh, Macoun, and Cortland are all good), peeled, cored, and thinly sliced

1/2 cup (55 g) roughly chopped walnuts, toasted

3/4 cup (165 g) firmly packed dark brown sugar

1/4 cup (60 ml) unsulphured molasses

1 teaspoon freshly squeezed lemon juice

1/2 teaspoon ground ginger

1/2 teaspoon cinnamon

1/4 teaspoon salt

Classic Pie (page 38) or Cornmeal Crust (page 44) for one 9-inch (23-cm) pie

Egg wash (page 25) or milk, for glaze

Vanilla ice cream, for accompaniment

Preheat the oven to 425°F (220°C).

Make the filling: Butter a large baking dish (9 by 13 inches is good, but you can use what you have), and spread the apples and walnuts along the bottom. In a large bowl, mix together the sugar, molasses, melted butter, lemon juice, ginger, cinnamon, and salt and pour them over the apples and nuts.

On a clean, floured surface, roll out the dough into any kind of shape, about ¼ inch (6 mm) thick. With a sharp knife, cut the dough into randomly sized pieces and layer them over the filling, allowing some to hug the sides of the dish. Make sure you leave some gaps for steam to escape. Brush the dough pieces with egg wash or milk.

Bake the pandowdy for 20 minutes, rotating the pan once halfway through. Lower the temperature to 350°F (175°C) and, using a metal spatula, push and chop some of the crust pieces into the filling. Bake it for another 40 to 50 minutes, until the crust is golden and the juices have thickened. Remove it to a wire rack to cool briefly until warm, about 30 minutes. Serve portions of the pandowdy with scoops of vanilla ice cream. The pandowdy can be kept for up to 3 days, covered in plastic wrap and refrigerated. Warm it in a low oven before serving.

APPLE-WALNUT PANDOWDY

I wanted to include this recipe for three reasons. One, pandowdy is a super-fun word and I like to say it as often as I justifiably can. Two, I am completely obsessed with Dinah Shore's rendition of the song "Shoo-Fly Pie and Apple Pan Dowdy," and had to include a pandowdy recipe as homage to her. Three, for those of you who are leery of rolling out perfect pie crusts, this recipe is as rustic as they come, and there's really no way to mess it up. And now, the chorus:

> Shoo-fly pie, and apple pan dowdy
> Makes your eyes light up,
> Your tummy say "howdy"
> Shoo-fly pie, and apple pan dowdy
> I never get enough
> of that wonderful stuff

MAKES one 9-inch (23-cm) pie

MOCHA BLACK-BOTTOM PIE

What goes better with coffee than pie (or vice versa)? Skip the cup of joe, and enjoy it in this rich, creamy, dark, and delicious pie. Black-bottom pies are another icon of Southern baking, and refer to pies with a bottom layer of very dark, barely sweetened chocolate topped by layers of light, chiffon-like custard. My version improves on the original by adding a dark shot of espresso.

MAKES one 9-inch (23-cm) pie

Chocolate Cookie Crust
(page 58) for one 9-inch
(23-cm) pie

FILLING

1 tablespoon unflavored gelatin

3 large eggs, separated

2 tablespoons cornstarch

1 1/2 cups (360 ml) milk

1 cup (200 g) granulated sugar

2 ounces (55 g) high-quality unsweetened chocolate, chopped

1/4 teaspoon salt

1 teaspoon vanilla extract

1/2 cup (120 ml) brewed espresso, or 2 tablespoons instant espresso powder

TOPPING

1 cup (240 ml) heavy cream

1 tablespoon powdered sugar

1 ounce (30 g) bittersweet chocolate, shaved or grated

Preheat the oven to 350°F (175°C). Pat the crust into a 9-inch (23-cm) pie plate. Bake it for 10 minutes, then let it cool completely.

Make the filling: Pour 1/4 cup (60 ml) cold water into a small bowl and dust it with the gelatin. Set it aside to bloom.

In a small bowl, beat the egg yolks. In a separate small bowl, mix the cornstarch with 1/4 cup (60 ml) of the milk until it is dissolved.

In a large, heavy-bottomed saucepan, heat the remaining milk over medium-high heat until it is scalded. Slowly drizzle a ladleful of the hot milk into the egg yolks, while whisking them constantly. Whisk the tempered yolks back into the milk, then whisk in 1/2 cup (100 g) of the granulated sugar and the cornstarch slurry. Whisk constantly and cook until the mixture is thick, about 5 minutes. Remove it from the heat.

Put the chocolate in a small, heatproof bowl and pour 1 cup (240 ml) of the hot custard over it to melt. Allow the chocolate to sit for 1 minute, then add the salt and vanilla and whisk to blend. Pour the chocolate custard into the crust and spread it evenly over the bottom. Refrigerate it to set while preparing the rest of the pie.

Whisk the gelatin mixture into the remaining custard along with the espresso and set it aside to cool to room temperature (you can expedite this by placing the bowl over an ice bath, stirring).

In a clean, dry stand mixer or mixing bowl, beat the egg whites until soft peaks form, then add in the remaining 1/2 cup (100 g) granulated sugar and beat until the meringue is stiff. Fold the meringue gently into the coffee custard, then carefully spread it over the chocolate layer in the pie shell. Refrigerate the pie, loosely covered in plastic, until chilled completely, at least 4 hours.

Make the topping: Shortly before serving, in a stand mixer, with a hand mixer, or by hand with a whisk, whip the cream with the powdered sugar until stiff peaks form. Spread the whipped cream over the pie and top it with the chocolate. Before topping, this pie can be refrigerated for up to 3 days, covered in plastic wrap. Make the topping just before serving.

BUTTERCRUNCH PIE

This recipe was inspired by my brilliant mother. Buttercrunch is an evil union of buttery, crunchy toffee with chocolate and salted walnuts. It also happens to be my mom's signature candy, and the first one she ever learned to make. I've been eating her delectable buttercrunch since I was a toddler, so it's basically in my DNA at this point. Obviously, I had to turn it into a pie. I've included the toffee recipe below, but you can also just buy some from my mom at Roni-Sue's (roni-sue.com) if you want to save a step!

MAKES one 9-inch (23-cm) pie

Classic Pie Crust (page 38) for one 9-inch (23-cm) pie

FILLING

$1/4$ cup ($1/2$ stick/55 g) unsalted butter

2 ounces (55 g) semisweet chocolate, chopped

3 large eggs

$1/2$ cup (110 g) firmly packed dark brown sugar

$1/4$ cup (60 ml) maple syrup (Grade B preferred)

$1/2$ teaspoon salt

1 cup (30 g) finely chopped walnuts, toasted

1 pound (455 g) buttercrunch toffee (recipe follows), chopped into small pieces

Egg wash (page 25) or milk, for glaze

Preheat the oven to 425°F (220°C). Roll out the dough into a circle about 11 inches (28 cm) in diameter. Transfer it to a 9-inch (23-cm) pie plate, trim the overhang to about 1 inch (2.5 cm), tuck the overhang under, and crimp decoratively. Blind-bake the pie crust until partially baked (see page 35); set it aside to cool. Lower the oven to 350°F (175°C).

Make the filling: In a medium pan, melt the butter, then stir in the chocolate until it is fully melted and combined. Whisk in the eggs, sugar, syrup, and salt until fully blended. Stir in the walnuts and toffee pieces.

Brush the pie shell edges with egg wash or milk. Put the crust on a baking sheet. Pour the filling into the crust and bake it for 25 to 30 minutes, until the pie has just set and is still slightly wobbly in the center. Remove the pie to a wire rack to cool completely, at least 1 hour.

This pie can be refrigerated for up to 1 week, covered in plastic wrap. Let it come to room temperature before serving, or warm it in a low oven. It can be kept frozen for up to 2 months: Cover it in plastic wrap, then in foil, and let it come to room temperature before serving.

RONI-SUE'S BUTTERCRUNCH TOFFEE

MAKES approximately 1 pound (455 g)

8 ounces (2 sticks/225 g) unsalted European-style cultured butter (such as Plugrá), plus extra for greasing the pan

1 cup (200 g) sugar

$^1/_2$ teaspoon kosher salt

Generously butter a rimmed baking sheet, making sure you get all of the corners and sides. In a cast-iron skillet, melt the butter, sugar, and salt over medium heat. Cook, whisking frequently, until the mixture turns a light tan color, 15 to 20 minutes.

Insert a candy thermometer and continue to cook, whisking constantly, until the mixture reaches the hard-crack stage, 305°F (150°C).

Using oven mitts, remove the skillet from the heat and immediately pour the toffee into the greased baking sheet. Allow it to cool completely. (If you want to score the toffee into even pieces, wait about 5 minutes after pouring the hot mixture and lightly run a knife over the toffee in a 1-inch/2.5-cm grid, repeating this process every few minutes to keep the score lines intact.)

Once the toffee is cool, break it up into chunks and use immediately, or keep it stored in an airtight container at room temperature for up to 2 weeks.

NOTE This recipe is just for the toffee filling, not for the full buttercrunch, which includes dipping the toffee pieces in chocolate and walnuts.

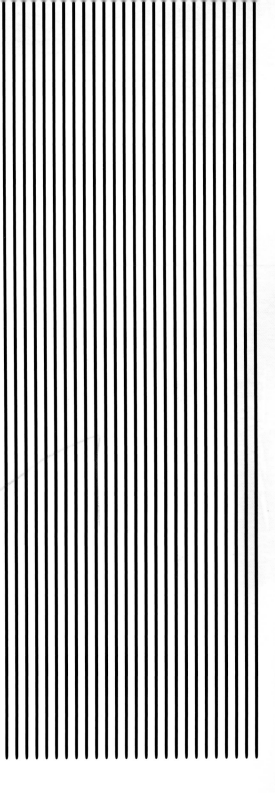

PEANUT-CARAMEL-APPLE PIE

Here we have a recipe inspired by one of my favorite after-school snacks. As a kid, I loved pulling fresh apple slices through mounds of peanut butter. Whoever came up with that combination deserves a statue in their honor. If I do say so myself, I think you'll be giving me some major kudos when you try this recipe, which elevates that childhood treat into a seriously grown-up dessert.

MAKES one 9-inch (23-cm) pie

Classic Pie Crust (page 38) for one double-crust 9-inch (23-cm) pie

FILLING

1 cup (200 g) sugar

2 cups (480 ml) heavy cream

1 cup (225 g) peanut butter (go for the natural kind; smooth or chunky is up to you)

$1/2$ teaspoon cinnamon

$1/4$ teaspoon salt

$1/2$ cup (70 g) whole peanuts, unsalted

2 to 3 pounds (910 g to 1.4 kg) large tart apples (Granny Smith, Rome, Mcintosh, Macoun, and Cortland are all good), peeled and thinly sliced

Egg wash (page 25) or milk, for glaze

Raw sugar, for garnish

Preheat the oven to 425°F (220°C). Roll out half of the dough into a circle about 11 inches (28 cm) in diameter. Transfer it to a 9-inch (23-cm) pie plate. Trim the overhang to 1 inch (2.5 cm) and refrigerate the crust.

Make the filling: In a large, heavy-bottomed saucepan, heat the sugar over medium-high heat. Let the sugar begin to melt, then whisk it lightly until it's fully melted. Allow it to caramelize, without whisking; just swirl the pan around occasionally.

When the sugar reaches a deep golden brown, remove it from the heat and carefully pour the cream down the side of the pan. Be careful: The sugar will sputter and release hot steam.

Return the pan to the heat and whisk until the sugar has dissolved into the cream. Whisk in the peanut butter, cinnamon, and salt until blended, then remove the pan from the heat. Stir in the peanuts, and let it cool slightly.

Lay half of the apple slices in the pie shell, pour over half of the caramel, then repeat with the rest. Brush the edges of the dough with egg wash or milk.

Roll out the second half of the dough into a circle about 11 inches (28 cm) in diameter. Lay it over the apple filling. Trim the edges, tuck the dough over or under the bottom crust, and crimp it decoratively. Cut steam vents into the top crust. Brush the crust with egg wash or milk and sprinkle it with raw sugar.

Put the pie on a baking sheet and bake it for 20 minutes, rotating it once halfway through. Lower the temperature to 350°F (175°C) and bake it for 30 to 40 minutes more, until the crust is golden and the juices are thickened. Remove the pie to a wire rack to cool completely, at least 2 hours. This pie can be refrigerated for up to 1 week, covered in plastic wrap. Let it come to room temperature before serving, or warm it in a low oven. It can be kept frozen for up to 2 months: Cover it in plastic wrap, then in foil, and let it come to room temperature before serving.

FILLING

1/2 cup (1 stick/115 g)
    unsalted butter

1 cup (220 g) firmly packed
    dark brown sugar

2 to 3 pounds (910 g to 1.4
    kg) tart apples (Granny
    Smith, Pink Lady, Macoun,
    and Cortland are all
    good), peeled, cored, and
    sliced into thick wedges

1/4 teaspoon salt

1 teaspoon vanilla extract

Classic Pie (page 38) or
    Cornmeal Crust
    (page 44) for one 9-inch
    (23-cm) pie

Vanilla ice cream, for
    accompaniment

Make the filling: In a large cast-iron skillet, melt the butter with ¾ cup (165 g) of the sugar over medium-high heat. Lay the apple wedges into the skillet in close, circular layers. Sprinkle the remaining ¼ cup (55 g) sugar, the salt, and vanilla over the apples, and cover the pan. Lower the heat to medium, and simmer for 15 to 20 minutes, until the apples have softened but still hold their shape. Remove the pan from the heat.

Preheat the oven to 425°F (220°C).

On a clean, lightly floured surface, roll out the dough into a circle ¼ inch (6 mm) thick and wide enough to fit your skillet. Lay the dough over the apples, and press the edges firmly over the edge of the skillet to seal.

Bake the pie for 20 minutes, rotating it once halfway through. Lower the temperature to 375°F (190°C) and bake it for another 30 to 40 minutes, until the crust is nicely browned.

Remove the pie to a wire rack to cool for 5 to 10 minutes. Run a knife around the edge of the skillet to loosen the crust. Press a clean dish or plate to the surface of the skillet (make sure it's larger than your pan), and flip them upside down to invert the pie onto the plate. The apples should release from the pan onto the crust, and should be nicely caramelized. If some of the apples stick to the pan, gently pry them loose with a spatula and arrange them back on the pie. If the apples are not as dark as you'd like, you can use a torch to caramelize them further, or put them under the broiler for a couple of minutes. Watch the broiler carefully to avoid burning the caramel.

Allow the pie to cool a bit, then slice it and serve, warm or at room temperature, with vanilla ice cream. This pie can be refrigerated for up to 1 week, covered in plastic wrap. Let it come to room temperature before serving, or warm it in a low oven.

WEST VIRGINIA SKILLET PIE

I came across this recipe in a great vintage tome, Delmer Robinson's *Appalachian Hill Country Cook Book*. The recipe might seem familiar: It's essentially a tarte tatin, that staple of French desserts. To my ears, West Virginia Skillet Pie just sounds better—but whatever you want to call it, you'll call it delicious.

MAKES   one 9-inch (23-cm) pie

Vanilla Wafer Crust (page 52) for one 9-inch (23-cm) pie

FILLING

4 large eggs, separated

²/₃ cup (130 g) sugar

¹/₂ cup (120 ml) freshly squeezed orange juice

2 tablespoons orange liqueur (such as Cointreau or Grand Marnier)

1 teaspoon pure vanilla extract

¹/₄ teaspoon salt

1¹/₂ teaspoons unflavored gelatin

TOPPING

1 cup (240 ml) heavy cream

2 tablespoons sugar

¹/₄ cup (60 ml) orange liqueur (such as Cointreau or Grand Marnier) or orange juice

1 teaspoon pure vanilla extract

Orange zest

Firmly press the crust into a 9-inch (23-cm) pie pan (see page 50). Chill the crust in the freezer or fridge while preheating the oven to 350°F (175°C). Bake the crust for 10 minutes, and then let it cool completely.

Make the filling: Put the egg whites in the fridge to keep cold. Beat the egg yolks with ⅓ cup (65 g) of the sugar until light and frothy. Beat in the orange juice, liqueur, vanilla, and salt. In a separate small bowl, sprinkle the gelatin over ⅓ cup (75 ml) cold water to allow it to bloom.

In a double boiler or in a metal bowl set over a pot of simmering water, whisk the yolk mixture constantly until it is slightly thickened and just coats the back of a spoon, 8 to 10 minutes. Remove it from the heat and slightly whisk in the gelatin mixture until it is completely dissolved.

Put the mixture over an ice bath or in the refrigerator, stirring occasionally with a spatula, until it reaches room temperature.

Once the yolk mixture is at room temperature, make a meringue. In a clean, cold metal bowl (copper is ideal), beat the whites until soft peaks form. Slowly add the remaining ⅓ cup (65 g) sugar and beat until stiff peaks form.

Gently fold the meringue into the yolk mixture in 3 to 4 batches, until it is fully incorporated. Be careful not to overdo it, so the chiffon doesn't deflate.

Pour the chiffon into the pie shell and refrigerate it for at least 2 hours.

Make the topping: In a stand mixer, with a hand mixer, or by hand with a whisk, whip the cream, sugar, liqueur, and vanilla together until stiff peaks form. Pipe or dollop the whipped cream onto the pie surface, sprinkle with orange zest, and serve. This pie can be made ahead, without the topping, and refrigerated for up to 1 week, covered in plastic wrap. Make the topping just before serving.

CREAMSICLE CHIFFON PIE

I've discovered something remarkable: There is a pie that tastes *exactly* like a Creamsicle. (Hint: It's this one.) I wasn't sure I could pull it off, but this pie turned out like a dream(sicle). (Sorry.) If you enjoy the light, sweet, creamy flavor of oranges and vanilla, this is the pie for you. Be sure to use freshly squeezed orange juice and real vanilla for the perfect flavor.

MAKES one 9-inch (23-cm) pie

November
(aka, pie month)

For us professional pie bakers, November is the Pie Olympics. Thanksgiving looms on the horizon and we plan ahead, stocking up on supplies and pre-ordering piles of pumpkins and apples. Here are a few of the recipes that I turn to year after year; the ones that I am happy to put on my holiday table.

■■■■■■■■■■■■■■■■■■■■■■■■■■■■■■■■■■■

BOURBON-GINGER-PECAN PIE

Classic Pie Crust (page 38) for one 9-inch (23-cm) pie

FILLING

1 cup (220 g) firmly packed dark brown sugar

1/2 cup (120 ml) real maple syrup (Grade B preferred)

3 large eggs, lightly beaten

2 to 3 tablespoons good bourbon (I use Maker's Mark)

2 teaspoons (about a 2-inch/5-cm piece) finely grated peeled fresh ginger (a Microplane is great for this)

1 teaspoon ground ginger

1/4 teaspoon salt

1 1/2 cups (170 g) pecan pieces

About 1/4 cup (43 g) crystallized ginger, finely chopped

Egg wash (page 25) or milk, for glaze

This is the pie that started it all for me. I've been baking this pie, in one form or another, since I was a teenager. Every Thanksgiving my family would get together in Vermont for a snowy holiday getaway, and my job was pie. Maple syrup was a lot easier to find in Vermont than the traditional corn syrup most pecan pie recipes call for, so I gave that a shot, with stellar results (grade B is more flavorful than A, if you can find it). At some point over the years, I started adding ginger—first dried, then a bit of fresh, and eventually I threw in some candied ginger for texture. The result is a pie that is sweet (but not too sweet), spicy, rich, and complex. Feel free to use a heavy hand with the bourbon—I sure do. When you try it, I think you'll know why it won first prize at the Brooklyn Pie Bake-Off.

MAKES   one 9-inch (23-cm) pie

Preheat the oven to 425°F (220°C). Roll out the dough into a circle about 11 inches (28 cm) in diameter. Transfer it to a 9-inch (23-cm) pie plate, trim the overhang to about 1 inch (2.5 cm), tuck the overhang under, and crimp decoratively. Blind-bake the pie crust until partially baked (see page 35); set it aside to cool. Lower the oven to 350°F (175°C).

Make the filling: In a large bowl, whisk together the sugar, syrup, eggs, bourbon, fresh ginger, ground ginger, and salt.

Put the pie crust on a baking sheet. Brush the crust edges with egg wash or milk. Add the pecans and crystallized ginger to the pie shell. Pour the liquid filling into the pie shell and bake it for 25 to 30 minutes, until the filling has just set and is still slightly wobbly in the center. Remove the pie to a wire rack to cool completely, at least 1 hour.

This pie can be refrigerated for up to 1 week, covered in plastic wrap. Let it come to room temperature before serving, or warm it in a low oven. It can be kept frozen for up to 2 months: Cover it in plastic wrap, then in foil, and let it come to room temperature before serving.

VARIATION
This pie can easily shoulder some chocolate! Just melt about 2 ounces (55 g) of bittersweet chocolate and stir it into the filling before pouring it into your pie shell.

PUMPKIN SPICE PIE

Thanksgiving is my second-favorite holiday (Halloween will always be number one in my book!), and naturally, the tradition of Thanksgiving pies is a big part of that. Any of the recipes in this month's section would be a relished addition to your holiday table, but if you're looking for a tried-and-true classic, look no further. This is one of the lightest, creamiest, most richly spiced pumpkin pies you'll ever taste. Serve it with a dollop of maple whipped cream for a truly autumnal treat.

MAKES   one 9-inch (23-cm) pie

Classic Pie Crust (page 38) for one 9-inch (23-cm) pie

FILLING

$^1/_2$ cup (220 g) firmly packed dark brown sugar

2 tablespoons all-purpose flour

$^1/_4$ teaspoon salt

$^1/_2$ teaspoon cinnamon

$^1/_2$ teaspoon ground ginger

$^1/_4$ teaspoon ground allspice

$^1/_4$ teaspoon ground cloves

$^1/_4$ teaspoon ground nutmeg

$1^1/_2$ cups (370 g) pumpkin puree (see Note)

$^1/_4$ cup (60 ml) unsulphured molasses

$^1/_4$ cup (60 ml) maple syrup (Grade B is best)

2 tablespoons dark rum (optional, but fabulous!)

1 large egg

1 cup (240 ml) heavy cream

Egg wash (page 25) or milk, for glaze

Preheat the oven to 425°F (220°C). Roll out the dough into a circle about 11 inches (28 cm) in diameter. Transfer it to a 9-inch (23-cm) pie plate, trim the overhang to about 1 inch (2.5 cm), tuck the overhang under, and crimp decoratively. Blind-bake the pie crust until it is partially baked (see page 35); set it aside to cool. Lower the oven to 350°F (175°C).

Make the filling: In a large bowl or the work bowl of a food processor or blender (the latter two yield lighter, creamier results), blend together the sugar, flour, salt, and spices. Whisk or blend in the pumpkin, then the molasses, syrup, and rum. Finally, blend in the egg and cream.

Put the pie crust on a baking sheet. Pour the filling into the crust and brush the rim with egg wash or milk. Bake it for 25 to 30 minutes, until the filling has just set and is still slightly wobbly in the center. Turn off the oven and open the oven door a few inches to allow the pie to slowly cool down for about 20 minutes (this helps prevent the custard from cracking). Remove the pie to a wire rack to cool completely. This pie can be refrigerated for up to 1 week, covered in plastic wrap. Let it come to room temperature before serving, or warm it in a low oven. It can be kept frozen for up to 2 months: Cover it in plastic wrap, then in foil, and let it come to room temperature before serving.

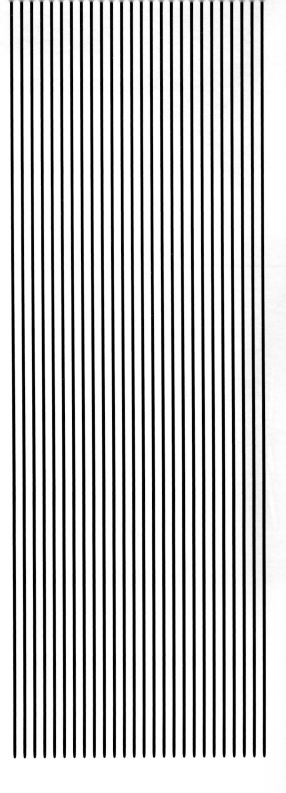

NOTE I like to use cheese pumpkins, sometimes called custard or pie pumpkins. Sugar pumpkins are great, too. To prepare them for pie, slice them in quarters and remove the seeds. With the skin on, rub them all over with a bit of olive oil and roast them at 400°F (205°C) for about 30 minutes, until the flesh is soft. Scoop the flesh out of the skins and put it in a colander over a bowl to drain the excess water, for a few hours if possible; overnight is ideal. If you're using a food processor or blender to make your pie filling, you don't need to puree the pumpkin flesh in advance. If you're whisking the filling by hand, it helps to puree the flesh beforehand.

If you don't want to deal with roasting your own pumpkins, the canned organic stuff works well too!

3-45
SECOND HAN

Vegan Pâte Brisée (page 46) for one 9-inch (23-cm) pie

FILLING

1 pound (455 g) soft silken tofu (not the vacuum-packed kind)

10 ounces (280 g) vegan bittersweet chocolate, melted

¼ cup (60 ml) nondairy milk (soy, almond, rice—it's up to you)

¼ cup (60 ml) dark rum or Kahlua (optional)

1 teaspoon vanilla extract

¼ teaspoon salt

TOPPING

2 (14-ounce/414-ml) cans full-fat coconut milk, chilled

¼ cup (20 g) powdered sugar

Shaved chocolate curls or toasted coconut, for garnish (optional)

Preheat the oven to 425°F (220°C). Roll out the dough into a circle about 11 inches (28 cm) in diameter. Transfer it to a 9-inch (23-cm) pie plate, trim the overhang to about 1 inch (2.5 cm), tuck the overhang under, and crimp decoratively. Blind-bake the pie crust until it is fully baked (see page 35); set it aside to cool.

Make the filling: In a blender, puree the tofu with the chocolate, milk, rum, vanilla, and salt until fully blended. Pour the filling into the cooled pie shell and refrigerate it until firm, at least 1 hour.

Make the topping: Spoon just the thick, almost butterlike cream off the top of the cans of coconut milk, reserving the coconut water underneath for another use (hello, piña colada!). In a stand mixer, with a hand mixer, or by hand with a whisk, beat the coconut cream with the sugar until fluffy and stiff. Spread it over the filling, garnish with chocolate shavings or toasted coconut, if desired, and serve. This pie can be made ahead, without the topping, and refrigerated for up to 1 week, covered in plastic wrap. Make the topping just before serving.

YOU-CAN'T-BELIEVE-IT'S-VEGAN CHOCOLATE-COCONUT CREAM PIE

I know what you're thinking: How on Earth can a vegan, dairy-free pie taste as good as one loaded with cream and butter? You'll read through the ingredients, you'll see coconut milk and tofu, and you'll want to turn the page. Stay your hand. Give this one a go, and serve it to the lactose-intolerant and vegans in your life. They will pester you to make this again and again, and you'll do so happily, because you'll love it too.

MAKES one 9-inch (23-cm) pie

CRANBERRY DREAM PIE

One of my favorite hobbies is collecting vintage, out-of-print cookbooks. They are such wonderful time capsules, reflecting both culinary and cultural trends of the era. My mom bequeathed me an amazing find: *The Lily Wallace New American Cookbook*, published in 1950. The recipes in this book are definitely of their time, and there's even a section in the back with planned menus for good nutrition, including sardine sandwiches, casseroles, and breakfasts of sautéed kidneys (like I said, of their time!).

Of course I went right to the pie section, and came across this gem—the name alone made me want to try it. I've modified it a bit to suit contemporary palates, and, believe me, when you taste it, you'll know where the name came from.

MAKES one 9-inch (23-cm) pie

Classic Pie Crust (page 38) for one 9-inch (23-cm) pie

FILLING
1 cup (200 g) sugar

4 cups (400 g) fresh cranberries

3 large eggs, divided, at room temperature

1 tablespoon cornstarch

$1/4$ teaspoon salt

1 teaspoon vanilla extract

1 tablespoon butter

TOPPING
$1/4$ teaspoon cream of tartar

$1/4$ cup (20 g) superfine sugar

Preheat the oven to 425°F (220°C). Roll out the dough into a circle about 11 inches (28 cm) in diameter. Transfer it to a 9-inch (23-cm) pie plate, trim the overhang to about 1 inch (2.5 cm), tuck the overhang under, and crimp decoratively. Blind-bake the pie crust until it is fully baked (see page 35); set it aside to cool.

Make the filling: While the crust is baking, in a heavy-bottomed saucepan, cook the sugar and 1 cup (240 ml) water over high heat until the sugar is fully dissolved and it just comes to a boil. Lower the heat to medium-high, add the cranberries, and cook, stirring occasionally, until they stop popping, about 10 minutes.

In a small bowl, whisk together the egg yolks, cornstarch, and salt until smooth. Temper the yolks by slowly drizzling ¼ cup (60 ml) of the hot cranberry syrup into the bowl, whisking constantly. Add the yolk mixture to the saucepan, whisking steadily. Simmer the filling for about 5 minutes, until the juices thicken. Remove it from the heat and stir in the vanilla and butter.

Make the topping: In stand mixer, with a hand mixer, or by hand with a whisk, whip the egg whites and cream of tartar until soft peaks form. Slowly add the sugar and continue to whisk until you have a glossy, stiff meringue (see page 19 for meringue techniques). Pour the hot cranberry mixture into the pie crust, dollop the meringue on top of the pie filling, and use a kitchen torch to brown the peaks, or broil it for a minute or two. Serve immediately.

APPLE-CRANBERRY PIE

I love cranberry sauce (the real deal, not the stuff that's shaped like a can). The combination of puckery-tart cranberries and aromatic orange is the perfect foil to the richness of Thanksgiving dinner. For this recipe, I wanted to find a way to combine those beloved flavors with a classic apple pie, and I think I've succeeded. The splash of Cointreau or Grand Marnier really pushes this one into the stratosphere!

MAKES one 9-inch (23-cm) pie

Classic Pie Crust (page 38) for one double-crust 9-inch (23-cm) pie

FILLING

$1/2$ cup (85 g) dried cranberries

2 tablespoons Cointreau, Grand Marnier, or orange curaçao liqueur (or orange juice for a non-alcoholic option)

$3/4$ cup (165 g) firmly packed brown sugar

Zest of $1/2$ orange

$1/2$ teaspoon dried ginger

$1/2$ teaspoon cinnamon

$1/4$ teaspoon salt

2 to 3 pounds (910 g to 1.4 kg) large tart apples (Granny Smith, Rome, McIntosh, Macoun, and Cortland are all good), peeled and thinly sliced

$1/2$ cup (125 g) fresh cranberries

Egg wash (page 25) or milk, for glaze

Raw sugar, for garnish

Preheat the oven to 425°F (220°C). Roll out half of the dough into a circle about 11 inches (28 cm) in diameter. Transfer it to a 9-inch (23-cm) pie plate. Trim the overhang to 1 inch (2.5 cm) and refrigerate the crust.

Make the filling: In a small saucepan over medium-high heat, cook the dried cranberries with the liqueur or juice until the liquid has been absorbed by the fruit, and set them aside to cool (alternatively, you can soak the dried berries overnight in the liqueur).

In a large bowl, whisk together the sugar, zest, ginger, cinnamon, and salt. Add the apples, fresh cranberries, and rehydrated dried cranberries and toss to coat.

Put the pie crust on a baking sheet. Fill it with the apple-cranberry mixture and brush the edges with egg wash or milk. Roll out the second half of the dough into a circle about 11 inches (28 cm) in diameter. Cut it into lattice strips or decorative shapes with a cookie cutter (see page 30) and arrange them over the filling. Trim the overhang, roll the dough under, and press it to seal. Crimp the edge into whatever pattern you like, brush the crust with egg wash or milk, and sprinkle raw sugar over the top.

Bake the pie for 20 minutes, rotating it once halfway through. Lower the temperature to 350°F (175°C) and bake it for 30 to 40 minutes more, until the crust is golden and the juices have thickened.

Remove the pie to a wire rack to cool completely, at least 2 hours.

This pie can be refrigerated for up to 1 week, covered in plastic wrap. Let it come to room temperature before serving, or warm it in a low oven. It can be kept frozen for up to 2 months: Cover it in plastic wrap, then in foil, and let it come to room temperature before serving.

Classic Pie (page 38) or
Cornmeal Crust (page 44)
for one 9-inch (23-cm) pie

FILLING

1 pound (455 g) sweet
potatoes

$^1/_2$ cup (110 g) firmly packed
dark brown sugar

$^1/_2$ cup (120 ml) grade-B
maple syrup or cane syrup
(Lyle's Golden is my
favorite)

1 large egg

2 tablespoons all-purpose
flour

$^1/_2$ teaspoon cinnamon

$^1/_2$ teaspoon ground ginger

$^1/_4$ teaspoon salt

2 tablespoons bourbon

$^1/_2$ cup (120 ml) buttermilk

$^1/_2$ cup (120 ml) heavy cream

Egg wash (page 25) or milk,
for glaze

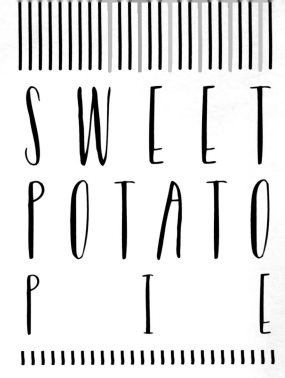

SWEET POTATO PIE

Preheat the oven to 425°F (220°C). Roll out the dough into a circle about 11 inches (28 cm) in diameter. Transfer it to a 9-inch (23-cm) tart pan or pie plate. Blind-bake the crust until partially baked (see page 35); set it aside to cool. Lower the oven to 350°F (175°C).

Make the filling: Roast the sweet potatoes for a more flavorful filling. With the skin on, poke the potatoes with a fork all over the surface. Put them on a foil-lined baking sheet and roast at 425°F (220°C) until soft, about 45 minutes. Allow the potatoes to cool, then cut them in half and scoop out the flesh, discarding the skin. You need 1½ (250 g) cups of flesh for the filling.

In a food processor, blender, or mixing bowl (a food processor or blender will yield the best results), puree the sweet potato with the sugar and syrup. Add the egg and process again. With the processor running, add the flour, cinnamon, ginger, and salt, followed by the bourbon, buttermilk, and finally the cream.

Lower the oven temperature to 350°F (175°C). Put the pie crust on a baking sheet. Pour the filling into the crust, and brush the rim with egg wash or milk. Bake it in the center of the oven for 25 to 30 minutes, until the filling has just set and is still slightly wobbly in the center. Turn off the oven and open the oven door a few inches to allow the pie to slowly cool to room temperature, at least 1 hour.

This pie can be refrigerated for up to 1 week, covered in plastic wrap. Let it come to room temperature before serving, or warm it in a low oven. It can be kept frozen for up to 2 months: Cover it in plastic wrap, then in foil, and let it come to room temperature before serving.

Most of us Northerners have pumpkin pies on our Thanksgiving dessert tables every year, but down South, they do some miraculous things with sweet potatoes, and this pie is proof. I adore its light, fluffy texture and the little taste of Southern sunshine it brings to my holiday table.

MAKES one 9-inch (23-cm) pie

December

One holiday leads to another this time of year, and we've barely finished our turkey leftovers before we're lighting menorahs and decorating Christmas trees. This also marks the beginning of the plethora of citrus fruit that will start traveling our way from Florida and the West Coast, lending a fresh brightness to our otherwise rich, hearty winter menus.

....

KEY LIME 182

SALTY DOG CHESS 183

MINCEMEAT 184

CHOCOLATE CHESTNUT 186

EGGNOG CREAM 188

KEY LIME PIE

Graham Cracker (page 54) or Gingersnap Crust (page 56) for one 9-inch (23-cm) pie

FILLING

1 (14-ounce/400-g) can sweetened condensed milk (organic preferred; get one that's only milk and sugar if possible)

$^3/_4$ cup (175 ml) Key lime juice (from 20 to 25 limes)

4 large egg yolks

Zest of 3 Key limes

$^1/_4$ teaspoon salt

TOPPING

Key lime slices, for decoration (optional)

Whipped cream, for accompaniment (optional)

There's something special about the fragrant, tart juice that comes from teeny-tiny Key limes. This is a classic recipe and I haven't done much to fuss with it. Use fresh Key lime juice if you can find it (you'll need a lot of those little limes to get the juice called for in this recipe, and a citrus squeezer will be your friend). If you have to use bottled juice, I recommend Nellie & Joe's brand, which you can find in the juice aisle of most supermarkets.

MAKES one 9-inch (23-cm) pie

Preheat the oven to 350°F (175°C). Pat the crust into a 9-inch (23-cm) pie plate. Bake it for 10 minutes, then let it cool completely. Leave the oven on.

Make the filling: In a large bowl, whisk together the milk, lime juice, yolks, zest, and salt until fully blended and frothy.

Put the pie crust on a baking sheet. Pour the filling into the crust and bake it for 15 to 20 minutes, until the filling has just set and the custard is smooth and not browned. Remove the pie to a wire rack to cool at room temperature for at least 20 minutes before refrigerating. Serve slices topped with thin rounds of Key limes and/or fresh whipped cream, if desired. This pie can be refrigerated for up to 1 week, covered in plastic wrap. Wait until serving to top it with whipped cream.

Classic Pie Crust (page 38) for one 9-inch (23-cm) pie

FILLING

4 large eggs

1 cup (200 g) sugar

Zest of 1/4 grapefruit

1 cup (240 ml) freshly squeezed grapefruit juice (Ruby Red will be sweeter and give a pinker hue; yellow grapefruit will be more tart)

1/4 cup (60 ml) vodka (or gin, tequila, or rum!)

2 tablespoons fine cornmeal or all-purpose flour

2 tablespoons melted butter

1/4 teaspoon salt

TOPPING

1 tablespoon high-quality sea salt flakes (like Maldon)

SALTY DOG CHESS PIE

Inspired by the eponymous cocktail, this pie amps up the flavor of winter grapefruit with a hit of vodka and a sprinkling of sea salt. You can substitute gin, tequila, or rum for the vodka with very happy results.

MAKES one 9-inch (23-cm) pie

Preheat the oven to 425°F (220°C). Roll out the dough into a circle about 11 inches (28 cm) in diameter. Transfer it to a 9-inch (23-cm) tart pan or pie plate, tuck the overhang under, and crimp decoratively. Blind-bake the crust until partially baked (see page 35); set it aside to cool. Lower the oven to 350°F (175°C).

Make the filling: In a large bowl, whisk together the eggs, sugar, and zest until light and fluffy. Whisk in the juice, vodka, cornmeal, butter, and salt.

Put the pie crust on a baking sheet. Pour the filling into the crust and bake it for 25 to 30 minutes, until the filling has just set and is still slightly wobbly in the center. Remove the pie to a wire rack to cool completely, at least 1 hour. Sprinkle the surface of the pie with the sea salt flakes just before serving. This pie can be refrigerated for up to 1 week, covered in plastic wrap.

MINCEMEAT PIE

Mincemeat pies, or mince pies, are pies served in the UK around Christmas. They were traditionally made with either suet, which is the fat around the kidneys of cows or mutton, or chopped, stewed venison. I know what you're thinking: meat in my dessert? But given the recent craze for bacon in sweets and confections, the idea seems less far-fetched.

I'm giving you two options: meaty or meatless. It's up to you; both taste delicious. If you decide to use suet, I recommend getting it from a good butcher who provides high-quality, grass-fed beef.

Note that the ingredients for this pie should be prepared at least 4 days ahead of time and can stay sealed in the fridge for up to 3 months. (Jarred mincemeat makes a lovely holiday gift as well!) As they sit, the ingredients macerate, which results in a more uniform flavor and texture.

MAKES one 9-inch (23-cm) pie

FILLING

2 large tart apples (Granny Smith or Mutsu), peeled, cored, and minced

¾ cup (130 g) dried cranberries

¾ cup (130 g) chopped dried dates

½ cup (85 g) pitted prunes, chopped

½ cup (110 g) firmly packed dark brown sugar

½ cup (115 g) shredded suet or melted unsalted butter

½ cup (120 ml) applejack, brandy, or rum

¼ cup (60 ml) freshly squeezed lemon juice

¼ cup (30 g) dried apricots, chopped

¼ cup (45 g) candied ginger, chopped

Zest of 1 lemon

Zest of 1 orange

½ teaspoon ground nutmeg

¼ teaspoon ground cloves

¼ teaspoon ground allspice

TOPPING

2 tablespoons powdered sugar

Classic Pie Crust (page 38) for one double-crust 9-inch (23-cm) pie

Egg wash (page 25) or milk, for glaze

Raw sugar, for garnish

Make the filling: In a large bowl, stir together all of the filling ingredients. Store them in an airtight container in the refrigerator for at least 4 days or up to 3 months.

Preheat the oven to 425°F (220°C). Roll out half of the dough into a circle about 11 inches (28 cm) in diameter. Transfer it to a 9-inch (23-cm) pie plate. Trim the overhang to 1 inch (2.5 cm), and spread the filling over the dough. Brush the rim of the dough with egg wash or milk.

Roll out the second half of the dough and use seasonal or holiday cookie cutters to cut out decorative shapes (you can opt for a lattice instead; see page 30). Arrange these over the surface of the mincemeat, brush them with egg wash or milk, and sprinkle the top with raw sugar.

Put the pie on a baking sheet and bake it for 20 minutes, rotating it once halfway through. Lower the temperature to 350°F (175°C) and bake it for another 30 to 40 minutes, until the crust is golden. Remove the pie to a wire rack to cool for at least 2 hours before slicing. Sprinkle it with powdered sugar just before serving.

This pie can be refrigerated for up to 1 week, covered in plastic wrap. Let it come to room temperature before serving, or warm it in a low oven. It can be kept frozen for up to 2 months: Cover it in plastic wrap, then in foil, and let it come to room temperature before serving.

FILLING

1 pound (455 g) chestnuts, or 1½ cups (360 ml) unsweetened chestnut puree

½ cup (100 g) sugar

2 large eggs

4 ounces (115 g) bittersweet chocolate, melted

1 cup (240 ml) heavy cream

1 teaspoon vanilla extract

¼ teaspoon salt

TOPPING

2 tablespoons cocoa powder (optional)

Classic Pie (page 38) or Chocolate Pie Crust (page 47) for one 9-inch (23-cm) pie

Preheat the oven to 425°F (220°C).

Score the chestnuts by cutting an "X" shape into the end of each one (this step is crucial). Lay them out on a baking sheet with the scored end facing up. Roast the chestnuts for about 30 minutes, until the skins peel open and the chestnuts are golden brown. Wait until they're just cool enough to handle, then start to peel them with a paring knife. The cooler they are, the more difficult they will be to peel.

Coarsely chop and set aside ½ cup (70 g) of the chestnuts. Place the rest in a medium saucepan and add enough water to almost cover them. Bring them to a boil, then lower the heat and simmer, covered, until they are tender, about 20 minutes. Keep an eye on the pan and add more water if needed. When the chestnuts are tender, puree them in a blender or food processor until smooth, adding water as needed to achieve the right consistency. You should have about 1½ cups (360 ml).

Roll out the dough into a circle about 11 inches (28 cm) in diameter. Transfer it to a 9-inch (23-cm) tart pan or pie plate, tuck the overhang under, and crimp decoratively. Blind-bake the crust until partially baked (see page 35); set it aside to cool. Reduce the oven temperature to 350°F (175°C).

Make the filling: In a large bowl, whisk together the chestnut puree and sugar. Whisk in the eggs, then the chocolate, and lastly the cream, vanilla, and salt.

Put the pie crust on a baking sheet. Lay the chopped chestnuts evenly in the bottom of the crust, then pour over the filling. Bake the pie for 45 minutes to 1 hour, until the filling has just set and is still slightly wobbly in the center. Remove the pie to a wire rack to cool completely, at least 1 hour. Dust it with cocoa powder, if using. This pie can be refrigerated for up to 1 week, covered in plastic wrap. Let it come to room temperature before serving. It can be kept frozen for up to 2 months: Cover it in plastic wrap, then in foil, and let it come to room temperature before serving.

CHOCOLATE CHESTNUT PIE

I've had the incredible good fortune to spend some time living in Paris, and one of my favorite memories is of strolling along the banks of the Seine in December, inhaling the delicious aroma of freshly roasted chestnuts. They sell them on the streets there in paper bags, and they put the hot pretzels of my hometown to shame. This pie is an homage to that sweet memory.

It's so worth it to make the chestnut puree from scratch: It keeps beautifully in the freezer, if you can avoid eating it all with a spoon! The process of roasting and peeling chestnuts is all about pleasure and pain: Your fingertips will be sore by the time you're done, but you'll be so thrilled to look down at a bowl of glossy, sweet, tender chestnuts that it won't matter.

MAKES one 9-inch (23-cm) pie

EGGNOG CREAM PIE

Confession time: I don't like eggnog. There's something about drinking eggs and cream that just doesn't sit well with me (no judgments though; if you like the nog, drink the nog!). I've discovered that most controversial foodstuffs are vastly improved when transformed into pie, and that certainly holds true for this love-it-or-hate-it holiday tipple. Be sure to use fresh nutmeg in this recipe—it makes all the difference.

MAKES   one 9-inch (23-cm) pie

Gingersnap Crust (page 56)
    for one 9-inch (23-cm) pie

FILLING

4 large eggs

1 cup (200 g) granulated
    sugar

1 teaspoon vanilla extract

$^1/_4$ teaspoon freshly grated
    nutmeg, plus extra for
    garnish

$^1/_4$ teaspoon salt

2 cups (480 ml) half-and-half

$^1/_4$ cup (60 ml) amber rum

$^1/_4$ cup (60 ml) brandy

TOPPING

1 cup (240 ml) heavy cream

2 tablespoons powdered sugar

2 tablespoons spiced rum

Pinch of grated nutmeg

Preheat the oven to 350°F (175°C). Pat the crust into a 9-inch (23-cm) pie plate. Bake it for 10 minutes, then let it cool completely. Leave the oven on.

Make the filling: In a large bowl or stand mixer, whisk together the eggs, granulated sugar, vanilla, nutmeg, and salt until well combined. Whisk in the half-and-half and liquors until just combined.

Put the pie crust on a baking sheet. Pour the filling into the crust and bake for 30 to 40 minutes, until the filling has just set and is still slightly wobbly in the center. Remove the pie to a wire rack to cool completely, at least 1 hour.

Make the topping: In a stand mixer, with a hand mixer, or by hand with a whisk, whip the cream with the powdered sugar and rum until stiff peaks form. Pile the whipped cream on top of the pie, and garnish it with a bit more grated nutmeg. This pie can be made ahead, without the topping, and refrigerated for up to 1 week, covered in plastic wrap. Add the topping just before serving.

January

It's a new year—time for new goals and aspirations. Perhaps you've resolved to spend more time in the kitchen this year? It's always good to create space in your life for quiet, contemplative recreation, and to me, pie baking is just that.

▪▪▪▪▪▪▪▪▪▪▪▪▪▪▪▪▪▪▪▪▪▪▪▪▪▪▪▪▪▪▪▪▪▪▪▪

Classic Pie Crust (page 38) for one 9-inch (23-cm) pie

FILLING

1½ cups (360 ml) apple cider

4 large eggs

¾ cup (150 g) granulated sugar

½ cup (120 ml) sour cream

¼ teaspoon salt

TOPPING

1 cup (240 ml) heavy cream

2 tablespoons powdered sugar

1 teaspoon cinnamon

Preheat the oven to 425°F (220°C). Roll out the dough into a circle about 11 inches (28 cm) in diameter. Transfer it to a 9-inch (23-cm) tart pan or pie plate, tuck the overhang under, and crimp decoratively. Blind-bake the crust until partially baked (see page 35); set it aside to cool. Lower the oven to 350°F (175°C).

Make the filling: In a small saucepan over high heat, boil the cider until it has reduced down to ¾ cup (180 ml), 15 to 20 minutes. Let it cool. (This step can be done ahead. The reduced cider will keep in an airtight container for up to 1 week in the fridge, or 2 months in the freezer.)

In a large bowl, whisk together the eggs, granulated sugar, sour cream, and salt until fully blended. Slowly drizzle in the reduced cider and whisk to fully incorporate.

Put the pie crust on a baking sheet. Pour the filling into the crust and bake for 20 to 25 minutes, until the filling has just set and is still slightly wobbly in the center. Remove the pie to a wire rack to cool completely, at least 1 hour.

Make the topping: In a stand mixer, with a hand mixer, or by hand with a whisk, whip the cream with the powdered sugar and cinnamon until soft peaks form. Pile the whipped cream on top of the fully cooled pie and serve. This pie can be made ahead, without the topping, and refrigerated for up to 1 week, covered in plastic wrap. Add the topping just before serving.

JAY'S APPLE CIDER CREAM PIE

You know that pie contest I mentioned back in the introduction? The one that rocked my world and launched my food career? Well, I wasn't the only one who went home a winner that day. My boyfriend, Jay, who insisted that I enter, who insisted I would win, took home a prize of his own! This recipe for his Apple Cider Cream Pie was voted Best Sweet Pie at the 2009 Brooklyn Pie Bake-Off, and when you bake it, you'll see why.

MAKES one 9-inch (23-cm) pie

MEXICAN CHOCOLATE PIE

Although I'm a New York gal through and through, I was actually born in Albuquerque, New Mexico, where I lived with my parents and our four dogs until I was two. During the decade that my parents lived there, my mom developed a serious taste for Southwestern food, and all the spicy chiles that go along with it. As a child, I couldn't handle the heat, but now I love it just as much as she does. At her chocolate shop, she has a whole chile-lover's collection of truffles for those who share our taste for the spicy and the sweet. This pie pays homage to her, and to the delicious flavors of Mexican hot chocolate.

MAKES one 9-inch (23-cm) pie

Gingersnap Crust (page 56) for one 9-inch (23-cm) pie

FILLING

8 ounces (225 g) semisweet chocolate, chopped or chips

1 cup (240 ml) heavy cream

1 large egg, at room temperature

1 teaspoon cayenne pepper (or to taste)

1 1/2 teaspoons ground ginger

1 teaspoon cinnamon

1/4 teaspoon salt

TOPPING

1 1/2 cups (360 ml) heavy cream

2 tablespoons powdered sugar

1/2 teaspoon cinnamon

1 teaspoon crushed red pepper flakes (or to taste)

Preheat the oven to 350°F (175°C). Pat the crust into a 9-inch (23-cm) pie plate. Bake it for 10 minutes, then let it cool completely. Leave the oven on.

Make the filling: Put the chocolate in a heatproof bowl. In a saucepan, heat the cream over medium-high heat until it is scalded but not boiling. Pour the cream over the chocolate and let it stand for 1 minute. Whisk together the hot cream and the chocolate until they are fully blended into a glossy ganache. Whisk in the egg, cayenne, ginger, cinnamon, and salt.

Put the pie crust on a baking sheet. Pour the filling into the crust and bake it for 20 to 25 minutes, until the filling has just set and is still slightly wobbly in the center. Remove the pie to a wire rack to cool completely, at least 1 hour.

Make the topping: In a stand mixer, with a hand mixer, or by hand with a whisk, whip the cream, sugar, and cinnamon together until soft peaks form. Pile the whipped cream on top of the cooled pie, sprinkle it with the pepper flakes, and serve. This pie can be made ahead, without the topping, and refrigerated for up to 1 week, covered in plastic wrap. Add the topping just before serving.

OATMEAL MOLASSES PIE

I love oatmeal. It makes you feel like you're being virtuous, even when you turn it into cookies (or in this case, pie) and toss in a bunch of chocolate and sugar and other delicious but not-so-virtuous treats. This pie has all the hearty, homey pleasure of an oatmeal cookie—but better. I decided to gild the lily and throw in some chocolate, but this easily adaptable recipe will gladly embrace whatever flavors strike your fancy. Feel free to add coconut, chopped nuts, or the chocolate of your choosing—it's all good! This pie is great with coffee, whipped cream, or ice cream.

MAKES   one 9-inch (23-cm) pie

Classic Pie Crust (page 38) for one 9-inch (23-cm) pie

FILLING

1 cup (240 ml) unsulphured molasses

3 large eggs, slightly beaten

4 ounces (115 g) dark chocolate, melted

2 tablespoons unsalted butter, melted

1 teaspoon vanilla extract

$^1/_4$ teaspoon cinnamon

$^1/_4$ teaspoon salt

1 cup (155 g) rolled oats (not instant)

Preheat the oven to 425°F (220°C). Roll out the dough into a circle about 11 inches (28 cm) in diameter. Transfer it to a 9-inch (23-cm) tart pan or pie plate, tuck the overhang under, and crimp decoratively. Blind-bake the crust until partially baked (see page 35); set it aside to cool. Lower the oven to 350°F (175°C).

In a large bowl, whisk together the molasses, eggs, chocolate, butter, vanilla, cinnamon, and salt until fully combined. Stir in the oatmeal and pour the filling into the par-baked pie shell.

Put the pie on a baking sheet and bake it for 25 to 30 minutes, until the filling has just set and is still slightly wobbly in the center. Remove the pie to a wire rack to cool until just warm or at room temperature before slicing and serving.

This pie can be refrigerated for up to 1 week, covered in plastic wrap. Let it come to room temperature before serving, or warm it in a low oven. It can be kept frozen for up to 2 months: Cover it in plastic wrap, then in foil, and let it come to room temperature before serving.

Classic Pie Crust (page 38) for one 9-inch (23-cm) pie

FILLING

1 (14-ounce/400-g) can sweetened condensed milk (organic preferred; get one that's only milk and sugar if possible)

4 large egg yolks

1/4 cup (40 g) pistachio paste (see Resources, page 220)

1 tablespoon orange blossom water or rosewater (see Resources, page 220)

8 green or white cardamom pods, seeds removed and ground

1/4 teaspoon salt

TOPPING

1/4 cup (30 g) chopped pistachios

2 tablespoons clover honey

1 tablespoon unsalted butter, melted

1/4 teaspoon salt

1 cup (240 ml) heavy cream

1 teaspoon orange blossom water or rosewater

NOT-QUITE-KULFI PIE

A couple of years ago, I had the chance to taste the kulfi ice cream from Adirondack Creamery, an artisan company run by Paul Nasrani, who makes some of the most incredible ice creams in town. Paul's father is from South Asia, where kulfi is a popular frozen dessert. For this pie, I've taken its key flavors and translated them into pie form. The whipped cream topping is made without sugar to balance the intense sweetness of the filling.

MAKES one 9-inch (23-cm) pie

Preheat the oven to 425°F (220°C). Roll out the dough into a circle about 11 inches (28 cm) in diameter. Transfer it to a 9-inch (23-cm) tart pan or pie plate, tuck the overhang under, and crimp decoratively. Blind-bake the crust until partially baked (see page 35); set it aside to cool. Lower the oven to 350°F (175°C).

Make the filling: Whisk together the milk, yolks, pistachio paste, orange blossom water, cardamom seeds, and salt until fully blended. Taste to check the balance of flavors; some spices may be stronger than others, so if it needs more cardamom or blossom water, add them to taste. Remember that the flavors will become more muted after the pie has baked.

Put the pie crust on a baking sheet. Pour the filling into the crust and bake it for 20 to 25 minutes, until the filling has just set and is still slightly wobbly in the center. Remove the pie to a wire rack to cool completely, at least 1 hour.

While the pie is baking, make the topping: Stir together the pistachios with the honey, butter, and salt. Spread them over a parchment-lined baking sheet and bake alongside the pie for about 10 minutes, until the nuts are dark golden brown but not burnt. Stir them halfway through baking for even cooking. Transfer to a wire rack to cool.

In a stand mixer, with a hand mixer, or by hand with a whisk, whip together the cream and orange blossom water until stiff peaks form. Pile the whipped cream on top of the cooled pie and garnish it with the pistachio pieces. This pie can be made ahead, without the topping, and refrigerated for up to 1 week, covered in plastic wrap. Add the topping just before serving.

GYPSY PIE

This pie came to me by way of Kent, in England, where it is a childhood favorite served at many school lunches. I'd never heard of it, but a friendly email from a fan across the pond brought it to my attention, and I was beguiled by its simplicity. It almost seems magical, the way these few ingredients come together. As with all minimalist recipes, the quality of ingredients becomes paramount. It's worth seeking out real muscovado sugar as opposed to turbinado or dark brown sugar. Its dark, aromatic quality gives all the flavor to this pie.

The lack of eggs or other binders means that air becomes an unlisted ingredient: When I tell you to beat it for 15 minutes straight, I mean it! Don't skimp on this step, or you'll wind up with a sad, runny pie. Chilling the milk beforehand helps as well. Be sure to let the pie cool completely before you try to slice it, and serve it with hot black coffee, tart berries, or unsweetened whipped cream to cut through some of that sugar!

MAKES one 9-inch (23-cm) pie

Classic Pie Crust (page 38) for one 9-inch (23-cm) pie

FILLING

1 1/2 cups (150 g) muscovado sugar

1 (12-ounce/340g) can evaporated whole milk, chilled (organic preferred)

1/4 teaspoon salt

Preheat the oven to 425°F (220°C). Roll out the dough into a circle about 11 inches (28 cm) in diameter. Transfer it to a 9-inch (23-cm) tart pan or pie plate, tuck the overhang under, and crimp decoratively. Blind-bake the crust until partially baked (see page 35); set it aside to cool. Lower the oven to 400°F (200°C).

Make the filling: In a stand mixer with the whisk attachment or in a large mixing bowl with a hand mixer or wire whisk (this is not a recipe for the weak of wrist, if you're trying it by hand), beat the sugar, milk, and salt together for a solid 15 minutes (at least!), until they are light and fluffy.

Put the pie crust on a baking sheet. Pour the filling into the crust and bake it for 10 to 15 minutes. The pie will not appear set and will have a sticky surface, but it will finish cooking as it cools. Remove it to a wire rack to cool completely before you attempt to slice it, at least 1 hour. The pie can be refrigerated for up to 3 days, covered in plastic wrap. Serve cold or at room temperature.

SALTINE CRUST

20 to 30 Saltine crackers (to make 1 1/2 cups crumbs)

6 to 8 tablespoons (85 to 115 g) unsalted butter, melted (Saltines can be very dry, so you may need more)

FILLING

3/4 cup (360 ml) heavy cream

6 ounces (170 g) cream cheese, at room temperature

3/4 cup (170 g) creamy peanut butter (if unsalted, add 1/4 teaspoon salt)

1/2 cup (50 g) powdered sugar

JELLY TOPPING

1 cup (225 g) all-natural jelly of your choosing (I'm a grape girl, but go with what you love)

1/2 cup (70 g) roasted peanuts, chopped

PB&J PIE

At Butter & Scotch, we serve up a trio of desserts called PB&J Three Ways. It's basically my idea of nostalgic heaven. PB&J (that's peanut butter and jelly, of course) is one of those timeless, perfect flavor combinations—and it's even better in pie form.

MAKES one 9-inch (23-cm) pie

Make the crust: Preheat the oven to 350°F (175°C). Grind the crackers in a food processor until finely ground or seal them in a plastic bag and crush them with a rolling pin. Pour in the butter and mix (hands are best for this) until the texture is that of wet sand. You may need more or less butter, depending on the dryness of the crackers.

Firmly press the cracker crumbs into a 9-inch (23-cm) pie pan (see page 50). Chill the crust in the freezer or fridge for 10 minutes. Bake the crust for 10 minutes, then let it cool completely.

Make the filling: In a stand mixer, with a hand mixer, or by hand with a whisk, whip the cream until stiff peaks form. Set the whipped cream aside.

Using the paddle attachment (or a wooden spoon in a mixing bowl), mix together the cream cheese, peanut butter, and sugar, starting on low speed and increasing the speed until the ingredients are fully incorporated. Scrape down the sides of the bowl, pour the whipped cream into the bowl, and mix again until all the ingredients are fully blended.

Put the pie crust on a baking sheet. Spread the peanut butter cream into the crust. Refrigerate it for 15 minutes to allow the cream to firm up.

Make the topping: Simply heat the jelly in a small saucepan over high heat until it just starts to boil and completely dissolves. Pour it over the chilled peanut butter filling, and return the pie to the fridge to allow the jelly to set. Garnish the top with the chopped peanuts. This pie can be refrigerated for up to 1 week, covered in plastic wrap. Serve cold or at room temperature.

Classic Pie (page 38) or Graham Cracker Crust (page 54) for one 9-inch (23-cm) pie

FILLING

4 large eggs

1 cup (200 g) sugar

1/2 cup (120 ml) sour cream

Zest of 1 lemon

Zest of 1 lime

1/4 teaspoon salt

1/2 cup (120 ml) freshly squeezed lemon juice (from about 3 lemons)

1/2 cup (120 ml) freshly squeezed lime juice (from about 4 limes)

TOPPING

4 large egg whites, chilled

1/4 teaspoon cream of tartar

1 teaspoon vanilla extract

1/3 cup (65 g) superfine sugar

LEMON-LIME MERINGUE

My version of a diner staple: This tart, sweet, creamy, dramatic-looking pie improves on the original by combining the bright citrus of lemons and limes (freshly juiced, of course) with a sky-high meringue that you can't wait to stick your fork into.

MAKES   one 9-inch (23-cm) pie

For the **Classic crust**, preheat the oven to 425°F (220°C). Roll out the dough into a circle about 11 inches (28 cm) in diameter. Transfer it to a 9-inch (23-cm) tart pan or pie plate, tuck the overhang under, and crimp decoratively. Blind-bake the crust until partially baked (see page 35); set it aside to cool. Lower the oven to 350°F (175°C). For the **Graham Cracker crust**, preheat the oven to 350°F (175°C). Firmly press the crust crumbs into a 9-inch (23-cm) pie pan (see page 50). Chill the crust in the freezer or fridge. Bake it for 10 minutes, and then let it cool completely. Leave the oven on.

Make the filling: In a large bowl, whisk together the eggs, sugar, sour cream, zests, and salt until fully blended. Slowly pour in the juices while whisking constantly, until they are fully incorporated.

Put the pie crust on a baking sheet. Pour the filling into the crust and bake it for 20 to 25 minutes, until the filling has just set and is still slightly wobbly in the center. Remove the pie to a wire rack.

Make the topping: While the pie is baking, in a dry, sparkling-clean bowl, whip the egg whites with the cream of tartar and vanilla until soft peaks form (this is easiest in a stand mixer). Slowly pour in the sugar and continue to whip until glossy, stiff peaks form. Pile or pipe the meringue onto the hot pie surface, and make sure it covers the entire filling, reaching all the way to the crust. Use a kitchen torch to toast the peaks and edges of the meringue. If you do not have a torch (get one; they're the best!), you can use the broiler to toast the meringue (see page 132). Just keep a close eye on it so it doesn't burn, and don't let it go for too long. Serve immediately.

February

This is the time of year when I most want to hole up indoors, hibernating like a bear and waiting for the sunshine to return. February is tough, but there are still some inspiring ingredients to be had and creative, whimsical pies to be made with them. This is the month when we most need those day-brighteners and mood-lifters, and I've got a few for you to try.

▪▪▪▪▪▪▪▪▪▪▪▪▪▪▪▪▪▪▪▪▪▪▪▪▪▪▪▪▪▪▪▪▪▪▪▪

SHAKER CITRUS PIE

Citrus fruit was a precious commodity back in the lean days when the Ohio Shaker community developed this recipe. True to their waste-not–want-not mentality, the Shakers utilized every part of the lemons in their original version of this pie—rind and all. In my take, you can use pretty much any citrus you like, as long as you take into consideration each fruit's particular qualities. The recipe below is for the classic lemon version, but check out the modifications that follow for different twists on this delicious classic, which is somewhere between a custard and a marmalade. This pie is wonderful warm or at room temperature, and pairs beautifully with coffee or ice cream.

MAKES   one 9-inch (23-cm) pie

Classic Pie Crust (page 38) for one double-crust 9-inch (23-cm) pie

FILLING

2 large lemons (organic if possible, but if not, use a fruit wash to thoroughly clean the skin)

2 cups (400 g) sugar

$^1/_4$ teaspoon salt

4 large eggs

$^1/_4$ cup (30 g) unbleached all-purpose flour

$^1/_4$ cup ($^1/_2$ stick/55 g) unsalted butter, melted

Egg wash (page 25) or milk, for glaze

Raw sugar, for garnish

Make the filling: In a large bowl, fully zest both lemons. Using a mandoline, vegetable slicer, or a *very* sharp knife, slice the lemons into paper-thin rounds (discard the ends of the lemons), removing the seeds as you go, and add them to the bowl with the zest.

Add the sugar and salt to the lemon slices and stir to coat them completely. Allow them to sit, covered, at room temperature for anywhere from 1 hour to overnight. The longer the slices sit in the sugar and salt, the more time the rinds will have to break down. For those who enjoy the bitter flavor of the rind, 1 hour is plenty of time.

When the lemons are ready, preheat the oven to 425°F (220°C). Roll out half of the dough into a circle about 11 inches (28 cm) in diameter. Transfer it to a 9-inch (23-cm) pie plate. Trim the overhang to 1 inch (2.5 cm), and refrigerate the crust.

In a separate bowl, whisk together the eggs and flour, then add the butter and whisk until it is fully blended. Stir the egg mixture into the lemons.

Put the pie crust on a baking sheet. Fill it with the lemon mixture, and brush the edges of the crust with egg wash or milk. Roll out the second half of the dough into a circle about 11 inches (28 cm) in diameter. Lay it over the pie, and trim the overhang to 1 inch (2.5 cm). Roll the edges of the dough inward or outward and crimp the edge to your liking. Cut slits in the top crust, brush the crust with egg wash or milk, and sprinkle it with raw sugar.

RECIPE CONTINUES

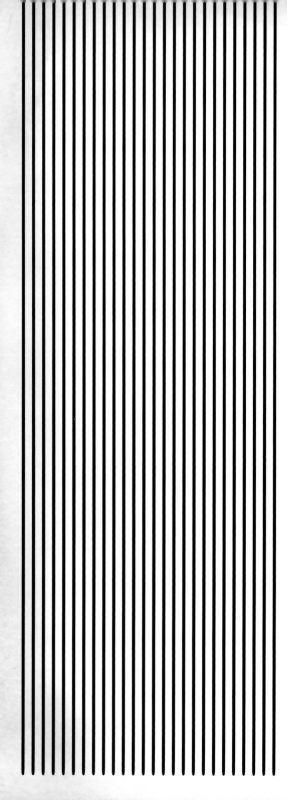

Bake the pie for 20 minutes, rotating it once halfway through. Lower the temperature to 350°F (175°C) and bake it for another 30 to 40 minutes, until the crust is nicely browned and fully baked and the filling doesn't jiggle under the crust when the baking sheet is moved. Remove the pie to a wire rack to cool for at least 1 hour before serving. This pie can be refrigerated for up to 1 week, covered in plastic. Allow it to come to room temperature, or warm it in a low oven, before serving. The pie can also be frozen for up to 2 months: Cover it in plastic wrap, then in foil. Allow it to come to room temperature before serving.

VARIATIONS

Grapefruit
Substitute 1 large grapefruit for the lemons. Zest it as in the recipe above, but remove the thick white pith around the fruit and discard it. Slice the rest of the fruit thinly. This version does not need to macerate in the sugar for as long a period of time; 30 minutes is plenty. As grapefruits are not as tart as lemons, only use 1 cup (200 g) sugar.

Lime
Substitute 4 limes for the lemons. Zest them as in the recipe above, but remove the tough rind from around the fruit and discard it. Slice the rest of the fruit thinly. This version does not need to macerate in the sugar for as long a period of time; 30 minutes is plenty.

Meyer Lemon
These fragrant lemons are not as tart as their everyday counterparts, so if you're lucky enough to find them to use with this pie, treat them exactly as in the recipe above, but cut the sugar down to 1 cup (200 g).

Graham Cracker Crust
    (page 54) for one 9-inch
    (23-cm) pie

FILLING

4 large eggs

1 cup (200 g) granulated
    sugar

$^1/_2$ cup (120 ml) sour cream

Zest of 1 lime

$^1/_4$ teaspoon salt

$^1/_2$ cup (120 ml) freshly
    squeezed lime juice

$^1/_4$ cup (60 ml) freshly
    squeezed orange juice

$^1/_4$ cup (60 ml) silver tequila

TOPPING

1 cup (240 ml) heavy cream

2 tablespoons powdered sugar

$^1/_2$ teaspoon salt

MARGARITA PIE

Inspired by the classic Margarita
cocktail, this pie is sweet, tart,
salty, boozy, and sure to cure the
worst winter doldrums!

MAKES one 9-inch (23-cm) pie

Firmly press the crust into a 9-inch (23-cm) pie pan (see page 50). Chill the crust in the freezer or fridge while preheating the oven to 350°F (175°C). Bake the crust for 10 minutes, and then let it cool completely.

Make the filling: In a large bowl, whisk together the eggs, granulated sugar, sour cream, lime zest, and salt until fully blended. In a measuring cup, mix together the juices and tequila, then slowly pour them into the egg mixture while whisking constantly, until they are fully incorporated.

Put the pie crust on a baking sheet. Pour the filling into the crust and bake it for 20 to 25 minutes, until the filling has just set and is still slightly wobbly in the center. Remove the pie to a wire rack to cool completely, at least 1 hour.

Make the topping: In a stand mixer, with a hand mixer, or by hand with a whisk, whip the cream with the powdered sugar and salt until stiff peaks form. Pile the whipped cream on top of the cooled pie and refrigerate it until ready to serve, at least 30 minutes. This pie can be made ahead, without the topping, and refrigerated for up to 1 week, covered in plastic wrap. Add the topping just before serving.

CRUST

4 strips good bacon (see Note)

10 to 15 (200 g) peanut butter cookies (to make 1 1/2 cup crumbs; see Note)

3 to 5 tablespoons (40 to 70 g) unsalted butter, melted, or bacon fat, or a combination of both

FILLING

5 large egg yolks

3 cups (720 ml) whole milk

2/3 cup (130 g) granulated sugar

1/3 cup (40 g) cornstarch

1/2 teaspoon salt

1 teaspoon vanilla extract

4 medium-ripe bananas

TOPPING

1 cup (240 ml) heavy cream

2 tablespoons powdered sugar

1 tablespoon creamy peanut butter

1 teaspoon vanilla extract

1/4 cup (35 g) peanuts (salted and/or honey roasted), chopped (optional)

Make the crust: Preheat the oven to 350°F (175°C). On a foil-lined baking sheet, cook the bacon until it is super crispy, but not burnt. Remove it from the oven (keep the oven on), and drain the bacon on paper towels. When the bacon is cool enough to handle, process it in a food processor with the cookies until you've got fine crumbs. Mix the crumbs with the fat until the crumbs are the consistency of wet sand. Press them firmly into a 9-inch (23-cm) pie plate and chill the crust until firm. Bake the crust for about 10 minutes. Allow it to cool completely.

Make the filling: Prepare an ice bath. In a small bowl, whisk the egg yolks lightly. In a large saucepan over medium heat, whisk together the milk, granulated sugar, cornstarch, and salt. Bring the mixture to a simmer but do not let it boil, whisking constantly for 4 minutes.

Temper the egg yolks by whisking them constantly as you ladle in a thin stream of the hot milk mixture. Add another ladleful of milk, whisking constantly, then pour the egg mixture back into the saucepan of hot milk as you whisk. Cook it over medium-high heat, whisking steadily, until the custard is thick and you see small bubbles breaking the surface, about 3 minutes. Remove it from the heat, whisk in the vanilla, and set the pan in the ice bath. Stir it occasionally with a spatula until fully cooled. (This can be made ahead and refrigerated for up to 1 day, covered tightly with plastic wrap. Make sure the plastic touches the surface of the custard, to prevent a skin from forming.)

RECIPE CONTINUES

ELVIS PIE

The King (otherwise known as Elvis Presley) was known for his swiveling hips, his dreamboat eyes, his smooth crooning, his ridiculous sequined jumpsuits, and his eccentric palate. One of his favorite snacks was a grilled peanut butter, banana, and bacon sandwich, which to some might sound obscene, and to others (me), obscenely delicious. This pie marries the sweet, smoky, salty, nutty flavors of Elvis's favorite sandwich in a rich, gooey, messy cream pie. Fresh banana pudding, topped with peanut-butter whipped cream in a peanut butter–bacon cookie crust. Need I say more? You probably only need to eat this once in a lifetime; you'll never forget it.

MAKES one 9-inch (23-cm) pie

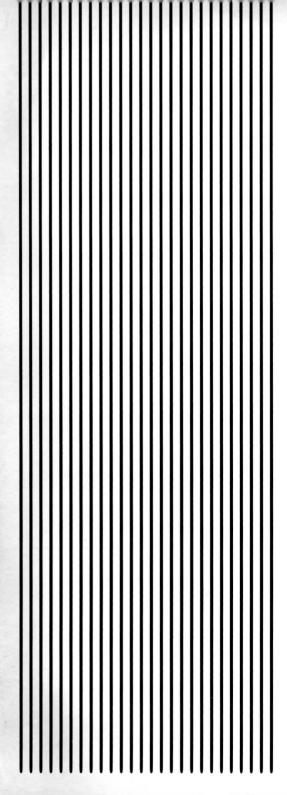

To assemble the pie, slice the bananas lengthwise or in circles, whichever you prefer, and arrange a layer of them in the bottom of your pie crust. Cover them with a layer of pudding, then repeat with the remaining banana slices and pudding.

Make the topping: In a stand mixer, with a hand mixer, or by hand with a whisk, whip the cream, powdered sugar, peanut butter, and vanilla until stiff peaks form. Pile the whipped cream onto the pie filling and top it with the chopped nuts, if desired.

NOTE Make sure the bacon is cooked very crisply so it doesn't become chewy. Use gluten-free cookies to make the entire pie gluten-free!

1. Layer fresh bananas on top of your crust.

2. Cover the bananas with a layer of pudding.

3. Top the filling with peanut butter whipped cream.

4. Garnish with honey-roasted peanuts.

HAMANTASCH GALETTE

Hamantaschen are my favorite Jewish desserts. These tricornered cookies are traditionally made to celebrate Purim, but I could eat them anytime. I've always felt that the cookie-to-filling ratio could favor the filling a bit more, and by transforming these little cookies into one big galette, a rustic, free-form pie, I've solved that problem.

Classic hamantaschen are filled with poppy seeds, prunes, or apricots, but go ahead and get creative with any jams, compotes, or jellies that you like. I've also heard tell of Nutella, halvah, dulce de leche, and even cheese hamantaschen—so go crazy! I'm including the poppy filling here as it's the most classic, and so tasty, but I encourage you to play around. Blow some minds at your Purim party with this striking, delicious dessert.

MAKES   one 10-inch (25-cm) galette

CRUST

12 ounces (340 g/approximately 3 cups) unbleached all-purpose flour

$1/2$ teaspoon baking powder

$1/2$ teaspoon salt

8 ounces (2 sticks/225 g) unsalted butter, at room temperature

$1^1/2$ cups (300 g) sugar

2 large eggs

2 tablespoons milk or orange juice

2 teaspoons vanilla extract

Zest of 1 lemon

Zest of $1/2$ orange

FILLING

$1^1/2$ cups (210 g) poppy seeds

$1^1/2$ cups (360 ml) whole milk

$3/4$ cup (150 g) sugar

$1/2$ cup (85 g) chopped dates or other dried fruit

Zest of $1/2$ orange

Zest of 1 lemon

1 tablespoon freshly squeezed lemon juice

2 tablespoons limoncello, orange liqueur, brandy, port, or other booze of choice (optional)

1 tablespoon unsalted butter

1 teaspoon vanilla extract

Egg wash (page 25) or milk, for glaze

Make the crust: In a large bowl, stir together the flour, baking soda, and salt. In a separate large bowl, beat together the butter and sugar until light and fluffy. Beat in the eggs one at a time, and then mix in the milk, vanilla, and zests until combined. Add the dry ingredients to the wet ingredients in two batches, stirring well halfway through, until they are fully combined. Wrap the dough tightly in plastic and chill it thoroughly, for at least 4 hours but ideally overnight.

Make the filling: In a spice grinder or coffee mill, finely grind the poppy seeds. In a saucepan over medium heat, cook the milk, sugar, dates, zests, and poppy seeds. Simmer them on low heat, stirring occasionally, until the seeds have absorbed the liquid and the mixture has thickened, about 15 minutes. Remove the pan from the heat and stir in the lemon juice, booze (if using), butter, and vanilla. Allow the mixture to cool completely. (This can be made ahead and stored in the fridge for up to 2 days, in an airtight container.)

RECIPE CONTINUES

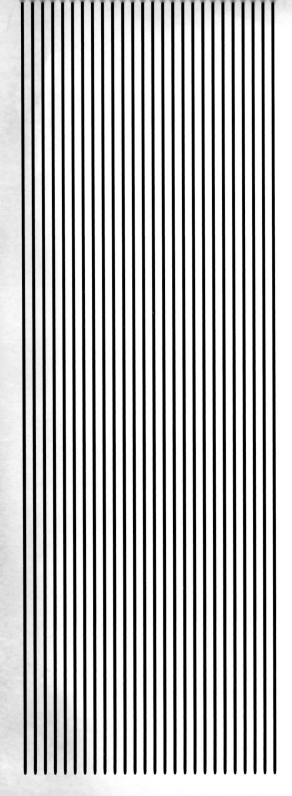

On a well-floured surface, roll the dough into a circle about 14 inches (35.5 cm) in diameter and ¼ inch (6 mm) thick (you may have extra dough; just use it to make small hamantaschen cookies with any extra filling or jams of your choice). Roll the dough back over your rolling pin to more easily transfer it to a parchment-lined baking sheet. Put the sheet in the fridge, uncovered, to chill the dough for 15 to 20 minutes.

Remove the rolled dough from the fridge and spoon the *mun* (poppy-seed mixture) into the center of the dough, leaving a 4-inch (10-cm) margin clear. Brush the edge of the dough circle all the way around with water or milk. Gently bring two sides of the dough together over the filling, pressing the edges firmly with the sides of your hands to seal them together This forms the top of your triangle. Then take the bottom edge of the dough and fold it inwards over the filling, pressing firmly to form the bottom of your triangle. You should be able to see the filling in the center. Go back over once more and firmly press with your palms to make sure the dough is well sealed along its seams.

Return the galette to the fridge for another 15 to 20 minutes, during which time you can preheat the oven to 350°F (175°C). Brush the dough with egg wash or milk, and bake the galette for 30 to 40 minutes, until the cookie crust is golden. Allow it to cool completely, then dig in! The galette can be stored at room temperature for up to 3 days, in an airtight container.

NOTE This dough is very finicky; it's best to let it chill thoroughly, ideally overnight, before you roll it out. Then it should be chilled in between steps to keep it sealed and beautiful throughout the baking process.

Gingersnap Crust (page 56) for one 9-inch (23-cm) pie

FILLING

4 large eggs, at room temperature

1 cup (200 g) granulated sugar

$^1/_2$ cup (120 ml) sour cream

1 teaspoon ground ginger

1 teaspoon grated peeled fresh ginger

$^1/_4$ teaspoon salt

$^3/_4$ cup (180 ml) carrot juice

TOPPING

1 cup (240 ml) heavy cream

2 tablespoons powdered sugar

1 teaspoon ground ginger

CARROT-GINGER CREAM PIE

Preheat the oven to 350°F (175°C). Pat the crust into a 9-inch (23-cm) pie plate. Bake it for 10 minutes, then let it cool completely. Leave the oven on.

Make the filling: In a large bowl, whisk the eggs with the granulated sugar until frothy. Whisk in the sour cream, gingers, and salt until they are blended. Slowly drizzle in the carrot juice, whisking constantly, until it is fully incorporated.

Put the pie crust on a baking sheet. Pour the filling into the crust and bake it for 25 to 30 minutes, until the filling has just set and is still slightly wobbly in the center. Remove the pie to a wire rack to cool completely, at least 1 hour.

Make the topping: In a stand mixer, with a hand mixer, or by hand with a whisk, whip the cream, powdered sugar, and ginger together until soft peaks form. Pile the whipped cream on top of the cooled pie or use a piping bag for a decorative design. Serve the pie immediately. This pie can be made ahead, without the topping, and refrigerated for up to 1 week, covered in plastic wrap. Add the topping just before serving.

If cakes can have carrots, so can pies! This was inspired by a pie I had the pleasure of trying at the Second Annual Brooklyn Pie Bake-Off. I was invited to be one of the judges after my own win the previous year, and we gave the Best Overall prize to a Carrot Chess Pie. Mine is a bit different in that it includes a good dose of ginger, which I love in general and find especially delicious alongside the sweet, herbaceous flavor of carrots. I think you'll find this somewhat unorthodox recipe surprisingly delicious!

MAKES one 9-inch (23-cm) pie

Classic Pie (page 38) or
    Cornmeal Crust (page 44)
    for one 9-inch (23-cm) pie

FILLING

1/4 cup (1/2 stick/55 g)
    unsalted butter, at room
    temperature

3/4 cup (150 g) sugar

1/2 cup (120 ml) barley malt
    syrup (see Resources,
    page 220)

4 large eggs

1/2 teaspoon sea salt

1/2 cup (70 g) malted milk
    powder

TOPPING (OPTIONAL)

1 cup (240 ml) heavy cream

1 tablespoon malted milk
    powder

1/4 cup (45 g) crushed malt
    balls

Preheat the oven to 425ºF (220ºC). Roll out the dough into a circle about 11 inches (28 cm) in diameter. Transfer it to a 9-inch (23-cm) tart pan or pie plate, trim the overhang to about 1 inch (2.5 cm), tuck the overhang under, and crimp decoratively. Blind-bake the crust until partially baked (see page 35); set it aside to cool. Lower the oven to 350ºF (175ºC).

Make the filling: In a stand mixer with the paddle attachment, cream together the butter, sugar, and syrup until fluffy. Add the eggs, one at a time, mixing well after each addition. Whisk in the salt and the malt powder until they are fully blended.

Put the pie crust on a baking sheet. Pour the filling in to the crust and bake it for 30 to 40 minutes, until the filling has just set and is still slightly wobbly in the center. Remove the pie to a wire rack to cool completely, at least 1 hour.

Make the topping (if using): In a stand mixer, with a hand mixer, or by hand with a whisk, whip the cream with the remaining malt powder until stiff peaks form. Dollop the whipped cream on top of the cooled pie. Sprinkle the crushed malt balls on top and serve. This pie can be made ahead, without the topping, and refrigerated for up to 1 week, covered in plastic wrap. Add the topping (if using) just before serving.

MALTED CHESS PIE

I've always loved the rich, nutty flavor of malt—in beer, in bread, in milkshakes, in pretty much anything. When I was first thinking up recipes for this book, my friend Delphine put in a request for a salty, malt-flavored pie, and I knew it had to be done. Most of the recipes out there for malted pies tend to be chocolate-heavy, chiffon-style pies. I wanted mine to let the pure malt flavor shine through, so I'm going with a chess pie—that classic pantry-staple recipe—to give you the full malt experience. It would not be gilding the lily to top this with a dollop of malt-scented whipped cream, but a cup of coffee would do nicely too.

MAKES one 9-inch (23-cm) pie

CRAZY PIEDEAS

Want to mix things up and get crazy with some pie? You've come to the right place. These absurdly delicious (and rather absurd) creations push pie to a whole new level.

PIE STACKS
(see pages 2 and 92)

Solitary pie slices are going to look pretty tame after you start exploring the world of pie stacks. The concept is simple: take two (or three, or four) pies with complementary flavors, stack them on top of each other, and slice away. It's a fun idea for a potluck where everyone brings a pie and you play around with flavor combinations. Here are a few great combos from this book:

- Trifecta & Banoffee
- Lemon Cream & Blueberry Nectarine
- Malted Chess & Mocha Black Bottom
- Toasted Coconut Cream & Pineapple
- Mint Julep Cream & Strawberry Rhubarb

The possibilities are endless!

PIE SHAKES

What's better than pie? Pie and ice cream. But, that doesn't have to mean a simple slice of pie a la mode. I heartily suggest making a milkshake, and in the last few seconds, blend in an entire slice of pie. Then grab a straw (and a spoon), and head on over to nirvana.

At Butter & Scotch we serve up some amazing pie shake combos, here are a few:

- Shaker Lemon Pie & Bourbon Sweet Tea Ice Cream
- S'mores Pie & Malt Ice Cream
- Trifecta Pie & Vanilla Ice Cream
- Banoffee Pie & Peanut Butter Ice Cream
- Mexican Chocolate Pie & Coffee Ice Cream
- Sour Cherry Pie & Ginger Ice Cream

Follow your palate, and pick whatever combination strikes your fancy!

ACKNOWLEDGMENTS

There have been so many who've helped and encouraged me through the long process of dreaming up, writing, and realizing this book—if I've forgotten to include you here, I promise to pay you back in pie.

My family and friends come first in the thanks department: Mom, for everything; Corwin, for always rooting me on; Dad, for believing in me; Jay, for your great ideas, unwavering support, and remarkable patience; Marlene, for your love and enthusiasm. Wendy, Corliss, Toby, Nick, Marli, Shoshi, Amber, Feiring, Kyle, Blessing, Molly, Laura, Julia, Legs, Rosie, Anna, Nate, Suzy . . . you guys kept me sane and reminded me that there's life outside of the kitchen. The Hawks: Jen, Carrie, Brian, Joe, Jess, Matthew—thank you for making my moonlighting period more than just a job. Keavy, thank you for inspiring me to grow, as a professional and as a woman, and for your endless stream of brilliant ideas.

Thank you: Holly Dolce, my warm, driven, and encouraging editor, who just gets it. It's been a huge relief to know that my book is in your expert hands; Natalie Kaire, for first believing in me, and Leslie Stoker, for shepherding me through a tumultuous time and making sure I never felt adrift; Alison Fargis, agent goddess, I worship you. (And thanks to Kimberly Oliver for introducing us!)

Many thanks to everyone at Stewart, Tabori & Chang who worked to edit, design, sell, and promote this book, especially Deb Aaronson and Cristina Garces in Editorial; Claire Bamundo, Erin Hotchkiss, and Marisa Dobson in Publicity; and Mary Wowk, Jody Mosley, Andy Weiner, and the entire Sales team.

This book wouldn't look so pretty without the skills of a few incredible women: Laura Palese, I actually felt like you were reading my mind when I first saw your design. You managed to intuit everything I wanted to convey—I think you might be magical. Thank you so, so much. Tina Rupp, your photographs make me want to eat my own pie, and since you know me, you know what a compliment that is! Mad props (ha!) to Leslie Siegel, for those gorgeous pie stands and textiles. Alison Attenborough and Hadas Smirnoff, thanks for teaching me your stylists' tricks, and for keeping me laughing through our shoot. Finally, thanks to all our pastry assistants for keeping us on schedule and whipping up some gorgeous pies: Claire Fishman, Yvette Hunter, Pearl Jones, Christina Lawhon, and Ashley Noble.

I'm so lucky to have had support from some incredible colleagues in the industry. Thanks to: Mitchell Davis, for your friendship and perpetual guidance; Rozanne Gold, for being an instant friend and mentor; Dorie Greenspan, for your unhesitating readiness to help, guide, and inspire; Liza de Guia, for telling our stories; Johnny Iuzzini, for your frank, invaluable advice (I swear I'll heed every word next time!); and Matt Lewis and Renato Poliafito, for spending an absurd amount of your valuable time detailing the ins and outs of cookbook-making.

Before there were finished recipes, there were testers: Ashley Melisse Abess, Keavy Blueher, Lexi Abrams Bourke, Ila Conoley, Brad Greenwood, Marlene Horton, Gina Hyams, Corwin Kave, Laura Kivlen, Lindsey Lambert, Melissa Locker, Debby Rabin, Karla and Scott Radke, and Ilona Williamson, thank you for taking the time to bake up early versions of these recipes, and for your feedback—it was invaluable.

And finally, my thanks to the readers of this book. I hope you spend many happy hours baking from it, and that its pages come to bear the telltale splatters, stains, and dog-ears of a well-loved, and well-used kitchen companion.

RESOURCES

Here are some of my favorite sources
for ingredients and tools.

Barley Malt Syrup
(for Malted Chess Pie, page 216):
Eden Organic (www.edenfoods.com)

Battenkill Valley Creamery
(www.battenkillcreamery.com)

Callebaut Chocolate
(www.callebaut.com)

Iwatani Butane Torch
(www.iwatani.com)

Kalustyan's,
for spices, herbs, and ethnic
ingredients (such as rosewater and
orange blossom water)
(www.kalustyans.com)

King Arthur Flour,
for flours and nut pastes
(www.kingarthurflour.com)

Maker's Mark Bourbon
(www.makersmark.com)

Martin's Pretzels
(www.martinspretzels.com)

Moho Chocolate
(www.mohochocolate.com)

Plugrá Butter
(www.plugra.com)

Polder Digital Thermometer
(www.polder.com)

Red Jacket Orchards
(www.redjacketorchards.com)

Rio Grande Organics Pecans
(www.riograndeorganics.com)

Roni-Sue's Chocolates
(www.roni-sue.com)

Sprecher's Root Beer
(www.sprechers.com)

Walker's Shortbread
(www.walkersshortbread.com)

Webstaurant Store,
for inexpensive, professional-grade
tools and equipment
(www.webstaurantstore.com)

INDEX

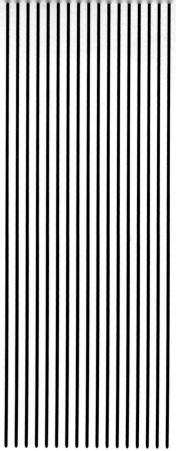

ALLISON KAVE

is the founder of the
made-to-order First
Prize Pies pie shop
on the Lower East Side.
In 2012 she and partner
Keavy Blueher opened
Butter & Scotch, a
dessert and cocktail
business based in
Brooklyn. She has
taught pie making at
the French Culinary
Institute and the
James Beard Foundation.